RAND NATIONAL DEFENSE RESEARCH INSTITUTE

T0306394

Leveraging Big Data Analytics to Improve Military Recruiting

Nelson Lim, Bruce R. Orvis, Kimberly Curry Hall

Prepared for the Office of the Secretary of Defense
Approved for public release; distribution unlimited

For more information on this publication, visit www.rand.org/t/RR2621

Library of Congress Cataloging-in-Publication Data is available for this publication.
ISBN: 978-1-9774-0342-1

Published by the RAND Corporation, Santa Monica, Calif.
© Copyright 2019 RAND Corporation
RAND® is a registered trademark.

Limited Print and Electronic Distribution Rights

This document and trademark(s) contained herein are protected by law. This representation of RAND intellectual property is provided for noncommercial use only. Unauthorized posting of this publication online is prohibited. Permission is given to duplicate this document for personal use only, as long as it is unaltered and complete. Permission is required from RAND to reproduce, or reuse in another form, any of its research documents for commercial use. For information on reprint and linking permissions, please visit www.rand.org/pubs/permissions.

The RAND Corporation is a research organization that develops solutions to public policy challenges to help make communities throughout the world safer and more secure, healthier and more prosperous. RAND is nonprofit, nonpartisan, and committed to the public interest.

RAND's publications do not necessarily reflect the opinions of its research clients and sponsors.

Support RAND

Make a tax-deductible charitable contribution at
www.rand.org/giving/contribute

www.rand.org

Preface

This report describes research and findings from a RAND study entitled "Recruiting Lab Study: Leveraging Data Technology and Best Practices for Youth Markets to Improve Microtargeting and Recruiting Outcomes." It is intended primarily for those who carry out and oversee military marketing outreach and recruiting.

Through the findings of this research, our sponsor sought to strengthen military recruiting by enabling the services and defense agencies and programs to more fully leverage new technological and methodological developments that allow other organizations to use data-driven outreach and recruiting strategies to microtarget individuals more likely to join and fit well with their organizations; address their interests, needs, and questions; and choose the right places and times to provide that information.

To accomplish this objective, we worked with the sponsor to identify and convene an advisory group of representatives from the services' recruiting operations divisions and marketing programs. They shared information on their strategies, practices, policies, databases, algorithms, and tools. With the sponsor, we also identified and convened a group of U.S. Department of Defense (DoD) Privacy Program and personally identifiable information (PII)[1] subject-matter experts (SMEs) to discuss the DoD Privacy Program, including related restrictions on data-enabled outreach and recruiting. Additionally, we

---

1 The Office of Management and Budget (OMB) defines *PII* as "information that can be used to distinguish or trace an individual's identity, either alone or when combined with other information that is linked or linkable to a specific individual" (OMB, 2016a, p. 33).

conducted focus groups with military recruiters concerning recruiting practices and challenges at the local level and reviewed business and academic literature describing use of data-enabled practices in marketing and recruiting. This report summarizes information we collected from stakeholders, SMEs, and the literature. We also provide actions that DoD can take toward enhancing use of data-enabled recruiting practices; these include evaluating the efficacy and efficiency of such practices.

This research was sponsored by the Office of Accession Policy within the Office of the Under Secretary of Defense for Personnel and Readiness and was conducted within the Forces and Resources Policy Center of the RAND National Defense Research Institute, a federally funded research and development center sponsored by the Office of the Secretary of Defense, the Joint Staff, the Unified Combatant Commands, the Navy, the Marine Corps, the defense agencies, and the defense Intelligence Community.

For more information on the RAND Forces and Resources Policy Center, see www.rand.org/nsrd/ndri/centers/frp or contact the director (contact information is provided on the webpage).

Contents

Figures and Tables

Figures

Tables

Summary

Background

Through data mining of large databases, recent technological and methodological advances enable use of data-driven outreach and recruiting strategies to help target prospective hires who are more likely to join and fit with one's organization; identify information concerning their interests, needs, and questions; and choose the right places and times to provide that information during their decision process.

While the military has had some success in applying these approaches, through the findings of this research, our sponsor, the Office of Accession Policy within the Office of the Under Secretary of Defense for Personnel and Readiness in the Office of the Secretary of Defense, sought to strengthen military recruiting by enabling the services and defense agencies and programs, such as Joint Advertising Market Research & Studies (JAMRS), to more fully take advantage of new technological and methodological developments.[1] Specifically, in concert with the sponsor, we addressed the following research areas:

1. What are the services and JAMRS currently doing in their recruiting efforts, particularly in using data-enabled outreach and recruiting practices that might be adopted more widely?

[1] JAMRS does not conduct recruiting; it conducts research that the services use in their recruiting efforts and responsible government offices use in their recruiting oversight functions.

2. How do organizations outside the U.S. Department of Defense (DoD) use big data and analytics for recruiting?
3. What additional data-enabled outreach and recruiting practices do the services and DoD want to adopt to build on those they currently are using and to leverage approaches such as those used in the private sector?
4. What are the barriers to adopting such practices?
5. What actions could be taken to facilitate data-enabled outreach and recruitment in the services and DoD?

Study Approach

To address these research areas, the RAND National Defense Research Institute worked closely with the sponsor and services to identify an advisory group of representatives from the services' recruiting operations divisions, current marketing agencies, and JAMRS and to convene a meeting of the advisory group members. The purpose was to share information on current strategies, policies, practices, databases, algorithms, and interactive tools being used in their outreach and recruiting. Our primary focus was on data-enabled outreach and recruiting practices in which individual services and JAMRS were currently engaging and that could be adopted more widely across the services, as well as on the related challenges to data-enabled practices that they reported.

We next (1) conducted focus groups with recruiters for the services to identify analogous strengths and issues at the local level and (2) reviewed business and academic literature describing the use of big data, machine learning, artificial intelligence (AI), microtargeting, customer relationship management (CRM), and interactive tools and applications in marketing and recruiting. The purpose of the review was to inform thinking about how DoD and the services might be able to further deploy big data analytics in their outreach and recruiting processes. We did not intend to identify one-to-one correspondences between the recruiting processes of the services and the private sector, given differences in the demographics of the populations targeted, the characteristics required for entry, recruiting operations, and privacy policies governing outreach and recruiting for military versus civilian jobs.

Finally, we again worked closely with the sponsor and services to identify and convene a meeting of key DoD Privacy Program and personally identifiable information (PII) stakeholders, including legal, privacy, and policy experts and relevant DoD and service representatives. The purpose of the attendees' presentations and related discussions was to look specifically at the DoD Privacy Program; implementation of this program; data collected by the services and DoD, with particular focus on PII; how digital information that includes PII is currently used for military recruiting purposes; additional data collection, data mining, analysis, and technological capabilities that the DoD Privacy Program and PII subject-matter experts (SMEs) believed would allow them to better use big data and PII; constraints to leveraging such approaches and data in military recruiting; and key actions that could be taken by DoD to facilitate such use of new information and technology in data-enabled outreach and recruiting practices.

Current Military Service Recruiting Operations and Uses of Data-Enabled Outreach and Recruiting Practices

Overview

Each service has its own specific outreach and recruiting practices, but the recruiting process for all services has many commonalities and works on two levels.[2] The national level focuses on outreach to develop an awareness of opportunities and to attract prospective recruits through service websites (i.e., goarmy.com, navy.com, airforce.com); advertisements on television, on radio, and in print; educational tours;

---

2 It was not within the scope of this study, or advantageous to the sponsor or the primary study audience that carries out and oversees military outreach and recruiting, to do a detailed review of the services' current recruiting practices. Rather, the tasks requested were to supplement routine interservice and DoD discussions of their outreach and recruiting methods by asking them to provide examples of data-enabled practices that might be more broadly applicable, additional desired data-enabled capabilities, and related barriers.

chat rooms; direct mail; call centers (1-800 numbers); and mobile tours and events (such as sporting activities or air shows). At the local level, individual recruiters conduct high school, cadet, community college, and other community programs or events; conduct other local outreach through personal contacts, emails, telephone prospecting, public service announcements, and other face-to-face encounters; assist walk-ins; and conduct interviews and discussions with prospective recruits attracted by national-level efforts.

Interested prospects who appear to be qualified are taken to a Military Entrance Processing Station (MEPS) for appropriate aptitude and physical tests. If they pass these tests, they can then meet with a military job counselor to discuss available jobs for which they qualify, review the enlistment options and training sequences for those jobs, and sign an enlistment contract. The current process is time consuming. For example, the Air Force reported that it takes it 110 contacts with different individuals to get a single recruit under contract and into basic military training.[3]

The types of data that the services reported collecting also had much in common. All services reported combining primary data collection with third-party data to help target recruiting activities. The level of detail and data-enabled practices at various stages in the recruiting process varied by service and stage, however. The services indicated that they collected only limited information from initial contacts, sufficient for a recruiter to contact the individual. Recruiters obtain much more detailed information during an initial interview that enables them to address qualification on factors such as age and education, finances, medical details, and social or conduct issues. Such information contains PII that must be protected. Data on aptitude and physical test results are added to the profiles of potential recruits who progress to the MEPS. The contact information for the recruiting lead and subsequent details are submitted to one or more centralized service databases.

---

3 *Contacts* here refers to interactions with youth who have expressed possible interest in serving through such means as responses to advertising, school programs, or direct mail; walking into a recruiting location; or referrals.

The services also revealed common challenges in meeting recruiting goals. They noted resource shortages in manpower, dollars, or both, and, as a result, they indicated that they were pursuing data-enabled efficiencies in their outreach and recruiting operations.

Use of Big Data and Analytics in Recruitment

Big data "is a loose description for the general idea of integrating large data sets from multiple sources with the aim of delivering some new, useful insight from those data" (Ridgeway, 2017). The availability of big data, advancement in AI, development of expansive information technology (IT) infrastructure, and increased computing power can be leveraged to transform outreach and prospective recruit management strategies. AI is defined "as the ability of a machine to perform cognitive functions we associate with human minds, such as perceiving, reasoning, learning, and problem solving" (Chui and McCarthy, 2018). In the advisory group and DoD Privacy Program/PII meetings, the military services and JAMRS reported some success in using data-enabled outreach and recruiting strategies to help locate youth who may be qualified for and interested in military service and to recruit them. The services and JAMRS felt that these strategies could be adopted more widely across the services. We note that a productive response from specific data-enabled outreach and recruiting strategies does not in itself quantify their efficiency relative to alternative approaches.

The services reported using data that they had collected to develop strategic recruiting plans, descriptive market assessments, messaging strategies, media strategies, and outreach locations and to provide insights for recruiters. The ultimate aim was to help recruiters achieve their mission—whether focused on generating leads, enhancing and scoring them, targeting locations and events, or prioritizing and shaping interactions with prospective recruits. The services also use the data to assess how well they are meeting annual goals and to provide insights on whether and how resources should be shifted to better attract recruits. Reserve components collect forecasts of separations from the active component to use in developing a cross-component retention mission, as well as a marketing strategy targeted to prior-service recruits who do not immediately join the reserve after leaving the military.

The services reported that they supplement their own data collection about recruiting markets with information from third-party sources and use the information to construct target audience profiles; help define the marketplace; and assess propensity to join, prior production, and market receptiveness. One third-party source used extensively by the services is DoD's JAMRS program. JAMRS provides market analysis that helps identify promising recruiting markets overall and for individual services, as well as information on how best to engage with youth in those markets, including their motivations and the most-appropriate touch points (social media, phone, cold calling, email). These analyses can help to produce minority accessions and high-quality accessions. JAMRS also provides targeted recruiting recommendations down to individual ZIP codes (Hall, 2017).

Some services reported using mapping applications that allow recruiters to visualize promising recruiting zones and location-specific trends. They also reported that use of social media is increasing at the national level to build brand awareness and encourage military service and at the recruiter level to address frequently asked questions and support peer-to-peer conversations.

Examples of Service-Specific Reported Uses of Data and Analytics

Service-specific uses of data and analytics discussed by the advisory group varied. Examples of how the individual services reported using data-enabled outreach and recruiting are listed below.

- The Air Force uses analysis to construct target audiences that shape prioritization, messaging strategies, and the selection of outreach tactics across touch points.
- The Air Force Reserve uses separation forecasts to feed strategic planning. It examines markets and accession mix to inform advertisements for specific types of people.
- The Navy generates monthly production reports, trend and risk analyses, relationships among data elements, and recruiting predictive tools. Production reports are used both as descriptive

summaries of historical data and for predictive and prescriptive reporting. The Navy's analytics inform much of its recruiting decisionmaking, including manpower and resource allocation, as well as program and process improvements.

- The Marine Corps analyzes recruiting success at various stages of decisionmaking to obtain "health of the brand" measurements.
- The U.S. Army Cadet Command uses predictive analysis to determine what recruiting campaigns are required. The analysis uses machine learning, cadet demographics, and surveys to examine past performance and inform recruiting campaigns. It is tailored for each school, each market, historical trends, and performance.
- The Army Marketing and Research Group uses analytic tools to select marketing venues based on specific goals, where to purchase media, and whom to target.
- The U.S. Army Recruiting Command uses analytics to inform planning of recruiting activities and identify priorities, including resource allocation, mission assignment, targeting, and advertising campaigns, to attempt to maximize return on investment (ROI) and mission success. The analytics include lead refinement models, prospecting activity optimization, and classification of "must win" and "must keep" markets. Prioritization is applied to ZIP codes and schools at the station level, and to larger markets at the company, battalion, and brigade levels. The goal is to focus on markets most likely to produce qualified, high-quality recruits.
- The Army National Guard uses predictive modeling to generate mission estimates.

The examples highlight several promising practices that could be expanded. A more general capability that the Army reported is its Virtual Recruiting Center (VRC), which includes a Leads Refinement Center (LRC). As leads come in, analytic models streamline those leads, confirming commitment and initial qualification, to save recruiters' time. Every lead is scored with a model; recruiters use the scoring to prioritize follow-up with leads. Each user entity is responsible for the validation of models. Supervisors and workgroups provide oversight. Internal Army modeling efforts are relatively small, are used for decision support, and are adapted routinely based on commander guidance.

The Army defines virtual recruiting as using digital methods to help find, influence, interview, qualify, process, and enlist or commission its future members. Virtual recruiting operations are carried out through digital systems using platforms such as email, the internet, and social media applications (e.g., Facebook, Twitter, LinkedIn, Snapchat). Virtual recruiting teams (VRTs) use only virtual recruiting processes to generate enlistments or commissions. Their activities include content creation and digital marketing analysis, supporting relationships with community partners, promoting and supporting Army events, and providing training and oversight to personnel in virtual prospecting, social media security, and regulatory compliance. Their objective is to generate additional high-quality leads for the battalion. Lead refinement accounts for half of their activities and is focused on producing new and improved lead sources. Social media posting, prospecting, and lead generation make up the other half of the VRTs' activities.

In the recent past, the U.S. Army Recruiting Command has significantly expanded virtual recruiting, adding VRTs in each battalion and a digital engagement fusion team in the headquarters. VRTs initially generate, screen, and prioritize leads for stations; create social media interest before events; train recruiters in the use of social media; initiate applicant processing; focus efforts on specific recruiting shortfalls; work to increase interest and appointments; and conduct online interviews.

Recruiter Practices at the Local Level

In our focus groups, recruiters indicated that they develop their own recruiting strategies and tools to effectively recruit in their assigned area, based on factors such as local interest in the military, reasons for or against joining the military, and local schools' openness to giving access to recruiters.

Recruiters try to gauge a youth's interest in serving and ability to qualify. They described prioritizing leads (i.e., individuals) and recruiting activities mostly in an ad hoc manner, according to initial screening or background factors that helped them assess interest and qualification. They reported that they largely prioritized which schools to engage with based on past success with the schools, their relationships with them, and how friendly they are to the military. Recruiters said that such priority rankings sometimes are passed down but said that they often adjust them. Recruiters also reported that recruiting events they were expected to attend were often prioritized in an ad hoc manner, rather than based on the ROI.

Use of Data-Enabled Outreach and Recruiting Practices Outside the U.S. Department of Defense

In organizations outside DoD, big data and related analytics are used routinely and extensively to help achieve two interrelated goals. The first is *marketing* (McAfee and Brynjolfsson, 2012; Chui et al., 2018)—reaching out to the right potential applicants to encourage them to apply to a company or for a specific job opening. Data-enabled outreach involves continually gathering information about potential applicants from a wide variety of sources, building profiles and unifying the information of potential applicants, and analyzing potential applicants' information at the micro (individuals and population segments) and macro (nation, regions, states, or ZIP codes) levels to assess their preferences and propensity to join the organization. Using this information and the analytical results, human resources professionals and marketers design and execute targeted marketing campaigns that include tailored messages to potential hires. The goal is to optimize the campaigns to resonate well with potential applicants.

Big data and analytics are also used in *recruiting* applicants (see discussion in the "Data-Enabled Recruiting of Good Leads" section in Chapter Three). The process begins by gathering information about good leads from a variety of sources and then scoring the leads on their probability of accepting a job offer and their suitability for the organization. Based on the information and estimated scores, individual leads are assigned to recruiters who are likely to work well with them. In the final step, recruiters execute the applicant management process to ensure that the best leads become applicants and accept the job offer. Throughout the process, recruiters provide personalized experiences by using a CRM system.

Achieving the desired results requires alignment of multiple factors: IT infrastructure, availability of data, suitable analytical models, and compliance in executing the new practices. For data-enabled outreach and recruiting systems to improve their effectiveness over time, they must be able to learn from the experiences of the users of the systems and prospective recruits.

Key Capabilities Desired by the Services and U.S. Department of Defense Programs to Better Use Data-Enabled Techniques in Their Outreach and Recruiting Efforts

Niche Targeting and Customized One-on-One Messaging

The SMEs stated that attracting and recruiting candidates for the all-volunteer force would benefit from broader use of data-enabled outreach and recruiting. They indicated that taking better advantage of third-party data and integrating it with their first-party data could enrich their marketing and recruiting operations, enabling them to develop deeper, more-granular target audience profiles. This would help them to prioritize prospective recruits and target them, including selection of media, touch points, and personalized messaging, and could support recruitment for specific career fields and jobs.

In part, microtargeting potential recruits through more extensive use of PII and third-party data involves cross-referencing data gathered from web measurement and customization technologies (WMCT) against PII. However, DoD agencies are regulated by explicit user consent or opt-in requirements and Office of Management and Budget (OMB) restrictions.

Another ability that the services expressed a desire to make broader use of involves text messaging. Although text messaging has become increasingly popular as a real-time, individualized communication and information exchange, the services reported uncertainty about its use for recruiting, even when the prospective recruit provides the mobile number, because it involves PII.

Experimental Assessment of the Potential Value of New Variables and Technology

An important desired capability is temporarily adding new variables or technology to a data collection effort so that their value can be assessed before changing the related System of Records Notice (SORN). The participants indicated that changing and obtaining approval for the modified SORN can be a very lengthy and time-consuming process. They reported that the process can be so lengthy as to prevent new variables or technology from informing time-sensitive decisions, or, if the variables' usefulness was untested, the lengthy process could waste valuable time and resources.

Information Technology Improvements and Cloud-Based Computing

The services voiced their desire for greater use of cloud technology to store and share information. For example, the Army discussed limits on its current data-sharing capabilities and the need for a system through which the active and reserve components could share data, including mobile access. A related desired capability involves a CRM platform to allow data to be accessed directly from a variety of hubs, including by recruiters to better enable job-specific recruitment and targeted messaging, media, and touch points to optimize their efforts. Recruiters indicated their desire for more-modern systems that could better support them; improve the efficiency of their work; and increase interconnectivity, mobility, and technology-based communication with youth, including updated technology and policies to reflect the role of social media and other technology-based communication used by youth.

Challenges to Using Data-Enabled Outreach and Recruiting Practices in U.S. Department of Defense Settings

We noted in discussing data-enabled outreach and recruiting practices that achieving the desired results requires alignment of multiple factors: IT infrastructure, availability of data, suitable analytical models, and compliance in executing the new practices, as well as feedback from the users of these practices and those reached through them (e.g., prospective and actual recruits). During the recruiting SME advisory group meeting, recruiter focus groups, and the DoD Privacy Program/PII advisory group discussion, the services and DoD reported challenges in using data-enabled approaches related to these areas. We summarize the main points from these discussions below.

Issues Associated with Using Personally Identifiable Information and Third-Party Data Under the U.S. Department of Defense Privacy Program

To assemble big data, organizations must merge databases by matching information about individuals from a variety of sources, including third-party data. As discussed earlier, in their recruiting activities, organizations outside DoD draw information from web behavior, other online behavior, and mobile and direct marketing interactions. Multiple first- and third-party sources are used to generate insights about demographics, psychographics, lifestyle, and media consumption for prospective recruits. When used by DoD and the services, however, PII must be protected in accordance with the Privacy Act and related implementation guidance. Relevant points from the Privacy Program and implementation discussion during the DoD Privacy Program/PII workshop are summarized below.

The U.S. Department of Defense Privacy Program

The Privacy Act of 1974 (5 USC 552a[4]) establishes a Code of Fair Information Practice that governs the collection, maintenance, use, and dissemination of PII that is maintained in *systems of records* by federal agencies, including DoD. OMB circulars provide implementation guidance for the Privacy Act for all federal agencies, and, within

DoD, a directive and regulation provide departmental implementation guidance.

The Privacy Act defines *records* as "any item, collection, or grouping of information about an individual that is maintained by an agency." A system of records is any group of records from which information is retrieved by the name or other PII assigned to an individual. Under the Privacy Act, federal agencies must publish SORNs in the Federal Register upon the establishment and/or modification of a system of records to provide public transparency of what data are being collected, why, and how those data are intended to be used. Intentions to share information outside an agency must also be recorded in the SORN.

Related Restrictions on the Collection and Use of Big Data and Personally Identifiable Information by the U.S. Department of Defense and the Military Services

The additional capabilities desired by the services and DoD agencies are impeded by Privacy Act (5 USC 552a[4]), OMB M-10-22 (*Guidance for Online Use of Web Measurement and Customization Technologies*), and DoD Instruction 8550.01 Section f(1)(b) ("Web Measurement and Customization Technologies") restrictions on

- collecting new data or using new technology without updating the applicable SORN
- tracking users' individual-level activity on the internet outside of one's DoD domain
- sharing data with other federal agencies, the DoD components, or other organizations without explicit consent from individuals
- cross-referencing data gathered from WMCT against PII to determine individual-level online activity.

The services have limited use of third-party data under PII policy, including opt-in (consent) requirements. Constraints on the use of third-party data (e.g., restrictions on third-party data that the services can purchase from data brokers such as Acxiom, LexisNexis, Experian, Equifax, and TransUnion) limit their depth of knowledge about which prospects and leads are most promising, how to tailor their interactions with these potential recruits, and where and how to market.

Often, data are limited to ZIP codes or higher aggregation levels. This impedes gaining a micro-level picture of propensity to join or potential recruits' interests and concerns.

The current CRM systems that the services use are also restricted by these DoD policies, which limit their ability to capture an individual's history of interactions across multiple touch points, and, thus, limit the services' ability to provide a personalized experience.

Data Limitations

In some cases, data limitations are a result of how the services internally organize their data collection and access. The Marine Corps and Navy explained how information that would be useful for understanding a recruit's experience from initial contact to contract is not fully accessible because of security, stovepiping (i.e., infrastructure design that limits information flow), and data entry issues.

Infrastructure Deficiencies

One of the infrastructure issues reported by the services is that many data sets are disconnected from each other—i.e., stovepiped. This can result in access limitations, potentially preventing valuable information from being used in planning and forecasting or in understanding why prospective recruits dropped out of the process. It also can require the same data to be entered into multiple systems, a significant issue that recruiters reported as wasting their time and limiting their mobility. The Navy indicated that eliminating such barriers would improve analytical integration across logistics, finance, marketing, and recruiting operations; increase the analytical support that could be provided to decisionmakers across the enterprise; and support efficient use of recruiters' time. Related issues were raised by the other services.

Recruiters noted their desire for more-modern systems that could better support mobility and flexibility and improve the efficiency of their work, characterizing upgrading and interconnecting current IT systems as a priority. The services all agreed that infrastructure upgrades would go a long way toward increasing recruiter productivity. At the same time, they recognized that resources would need to be expended for such upgrades.

Analytical Tools

Recruiters reported lacking advanced analytical tools. They indicated that available tools focused on tracking leads or applicants through the recruiting process. The tools that recruiters described did not prioritize individuals, leads, activities, or events based on their ROI. Recruiters reported that even when efforts have been made to provide more mobile devices, their functionality was outdated, and the devices were not helpful.

Historical Trends Driving Current Practices

The services' advisory group presentations discussed their tendency to focus recruiting efforts in areas where they have been successful in the past, such as regional markets or particular schools. While this approach is logical and has been relatively successful in meeting accession targets, Census information indicates ongoing changes in youth demographics, and youth interests and career plans have changed over the years, as reported by numerous sources. Such changes may make traditional approaches less successful in the future. The services also noted shifts in the population distribution from more-rural areas to urban and suburban centers. This geographical shift may most directly affect the reserve components (which recruit for local units) but ultimately could affect all components because relocation from more- to less-isolated areas may present more alternatives for youth to consider. The Marine Corps talked about its need to expand its target audience through different messaging focused less on warfighting and more on humanitarian missions.

Lack of Feedback

The services talked about how lack of feedback on the success of outreach and recruiting operations constrains their ability to improve recruiting processes. They desired such feedback to develop more-granular target audience profiles, identify more-desirable prospective recruits, and use more-refined touch point selection to reach those audiences and prospects. They reported challenges in synchronizing efforts from the national to the local levels, including a mechanism by which insights from recruiters can be incorporated into forecasting.

They also wanted more feedback from potential and recent recruits on what is working well and what is not. The types of infrastructure deficiencies discussed above play a role in the lack of feedback.

Key Actions to Facilitate Use of Data-Enabled Outreach and Recruitment Practices in the U.S. Department of Defense

Continue to Share Information Across the Services, the U.S. Department of Defense, and Marketing Agencies About Their Data-Enabled Outreach and Recruiting Practices to Broaden Their Use

During the advisory group and DoD Privacy Program/PII meetings, the services indicated that they were pursuing data-enabled efficiencies in their marketing and recruiting operations by using data analytics to inform outreach and recruiting activities. Such practices included using mapping applications to allow recruiters to visualize promising recruiting zones and location-specific trends. They reported increased use of social media to develop a presence at the service and recruiter levels. Individual recruiters build virtual networks, gain a following, and follow others to create an authentic view of military service and, thereby, encourage joining. To save recruiters' time, the Army's LRC prequalifies leads and scores them on multiple dimensions, enabling recruiters to use the scores to prioritize leads for follow-up. The Army's VRC and VRTs support local recruiting efforts and can be used to target individuals or groups to fill specific needs. Wider adoption of emerging data-enabled outreach and recruiting practices would also reduce dependence on historical practices.

Improve the Interconnectivity of Information Technology Systems, Recruiting Databases, and Tools

Numerous participants in this research noted the utility of improving the interconnectivity of IT systems, recruiting databases, and tools. They reported that lack of interconnectivity can limit visibility of important data within and between echelons and functions, which, in turn, can cause duplication of effort, limit recruiters' time to engage in recruiting activities, and impede assessment and adoption of best outreach and recruiting activities. Moreover, the DoD Privacy Program/PII experts noted that many of the people, influencers, and prospective recruits that recruiters talk to are in the .com and .edu worlds. They thought it important to enable recruiters to reach such people securely and in an up-to-date communication format; this involves both PII and IT issues. Thus, near-term investments in IT upgrades and interconnectivity and in tools for recruiting (some of which would require IT and interconnectivity upgrades) could have a substantial ROI. DoD should address which of these investments are most critical and which are most actionable with respect to associated cost and technological issues.

Increase Feedback Within the Outreach and Recruiting Processes

The services wanted improved feedback to help develop more-granular target audience profiles, identify more-desirable prospective recruits, use more-refined touch point selection to reach those audiences and prospects, synchronize efforts from the national to the local levels, incorporate insights from recruiters into forecasting, and use feedback from potential and recent recruits on what is working well and what is not. The types of data and infrastructure deficiencies discussed above play a role in the lack of feedback.

Introduce Greater Flexibility into the System of Records Notice Development Process

Adjusting the SORN development process to be broader and more flexible could have considerable value in supporting data-enabled outreach and recruiting. The DoD Privacy Program/PII SMEs reported that the current SORN process is very restrictive in today's environment. They said that there are times when an additional variable or tool might have temporary value or long-term value not fully apparent without assessment, noting the value of a process to temporarily test something's value before having to go through the full effort required to change the SORN. They indicated that this could be accomplished by adding a routine uses phrase to SORNs that covered additional data and methods for mining and market research. Generic language could be used to allow for collecting data for testing purposes or testing new tools—in essence, to support experimentation. Another approach discussed was whether a broad SORN could be written for all DoD components and services to cover routine data collection and uses. This would provide more flexibility and reduce the services' workload but would require DoD to consider what level of joint recruiting it wants. Because developing such an approach would be time consuming, explicit steps to assess feasibility would be appropriate.

Target Impediments to Using Third-Party Data and Personally Identifiable Information in Marketing and Recruiting

Another important action discussed by the DoD Privacy Program/PII SMEs is to address existing statutes and policies that hamper DoD in taking advantage of third-party data and analytics. These restrictions focus on several areas: (1) collecting data beyond the directory level, (2) tracking individual users outside of one's domain, (3) sharing data that DoD collects or tracks or sharing behavioral data without consent, and (4) cross-referencing web users' behavior. The SMEs indicated that a change in authorities is needed to allow DoD to directly collect data beyond the directory level, as well as to more fully use external sources and third-party data and to share individual lead and prospective recruit data with those third parties, so that they can then share more-complete data and analyses with DoD. With better access to such data and analytics, particularly about what youth were doing prior to becoming prospective recruits, the services can better target potential recruits and customize the information provided to them. For DoD recruiting programs and the services to take full advantage of big data and machine learning, Congress, OMB, and DoD would need to broaden their authority to use those techniques and technologies. One approach could be for DoD to request a change in the applicable statute, OMB guidance, and DoD policies that would allow the services and DoD military recruiting programs to use marketing and recruiting practices employed outside DoD, such as those used in private industry. An initial, more-limited step could be for DoD to request authority to allow the services and programs to conduct pilot tests to investigate viable uses of third-party data and analytics, which would allow it to build the business case for broader changes.

Routinely Evaluate the Effectiveness, Efficiency, and Acceptance of Data-Enabled Outreach and Recruiting Practices in Military Recruiting

The efficiency and effectiveness of data-enabled outreach and recruiting practices in increasing leads or converting more leads into military recruits is relatively unknown compared with other areas, such as political campaigns (Nickerson and Rogers, 2014). Assuming that these practices have analogous positive effects on recruiting outcomes, improvements in IT infrastructure or analytical capabilities, if necessary, might nonetheless be costly, and the quality and characteristics of these leads and recruits should be assessed. Finally, to ensure their successful implementation, the services need to prepare recruiters to effectively use new tools in their daily work, and the reactions of members of the targeted population to ongoing data-enabled military outreach and recruiting practices should be routinely assessed.

Acknowledgments

We wish to thank our sponsors for their support throughout the study. In particular, we would like to thank Stephanie Miller (director), Christopher Arendt (deputy director), Dennis Drogo (assistant director), and Evelyn Dyer, Office of Accession Policy, within the Office of the Under Secretary of Defense for Personnel and Readiness. We also would like to thank our reviewers, Luke Matthews and David Knapp, RAND, and Alan Gelder, Institute for Defense Analyses (IDA), as well as Katherine Helland, Joint Advertising Market Research & Studies, and Matthew Goldberg, IDA, for their contributions over the course of the study.

We wish to express our sincere gratitude to the members of the recruiting advisory group expert panel, the U.S. Department of Defense Privacy Program/Personally Identifiable Information expert panel, and the recruiters from all services and components who participated in our focus groups.

At RAND, we are grateful to Lisa Kraus, Molly Doyle, Sarah Weilant, and Monica Mean for their detailed notes on the subject-matter expert (SME) discussions and recruiter focus groups; to Tameesha P. Coatney, Lt Col, U.S. Air Force, who provided the material for Appendix B; to Clara Aranibar for her assistance in arranging and supporting the SME meetings; and to Jerry Sollinger, Katheryn Giglio, and Barbara Bicksler for their assistance with earlier versions of this report.

Acknowledgments

Abbreviations

AFQT	Armed Forces Qualification Test
AFRISS-TF	Air Force Recruiting Information Support System–Total Force
AFRS	Air Force Recruiting Service
AI	artificial intelligence
AIE	Accessions Information Environment
AMRG	Army Marketing and Research Group
ANG	Air National Guard
ARNG	Army National Guard
ASVAB	Armed Services Vocational Aptitude Battery
BMT	basic military training
COI	center of influence
CRM	customer relationship management
DEP	Delayed Entry Program
DMDC	Defense Manpower Data Center
DoD	U.S. Department of Defense
EST	Enlisted Screening Test

ETAV	Enterprise Total Asset Visibility
HQ AFRS	Headquarters, Air Force Recruiting Service
HR	human resources
IDA	Institute for Defense Analyses
IT	information technology
JAMRS	Joint Advertising Market Research & Studies
LRC	Leads Refinement Center
MEPS	Military Entrance Processing Station
MORS	Military Operations Research Symposium
NALTS	National Advertising Lead Tracking System
NASCAR	National Association for Stock Car Auto Racing
NDRI	National Defense Research Institute
OMB	Office of Management and Budget
OSD	Office of the Secretary of Defense
PII	personally identifiable information
PSA	public service announcement
RIC	recruiter
ROI	return on investment
ROTC	Reserve Officers' Training Corps
SLA	service-level agreement
SORN	System of Records Notice
STEM	science, technology, engineering, and mathematics
SME	subject-matter expert
TRADOC	Training and Doctrine Command

USACC	U.S. Army Cadet Command
USAREC	U.S. Army Recruiting Command
USC	United States Code
VRC	Virtual Recruiting Center
VRT	virtual recruiting team
WMCT	web measurement and customization technologies

CHAPTER ONE

Introduction

The availability of big data, advancement in artificial intelligence (AI), development of expansive information technology (IT) infrastructure, and increased computing power have transformed business strategies and practices in the 21st century (McAfee and Brynjolfsson, 2012). The transformation has been most sweeping in the areas of marketing (Chui et al., 2018) and recruiting (see discussion in the "Data-Enabled Recruiting of Good Leads" section in Chapter Three). In recent years, technological and methodological advances have enabled organizations to use evidence-driven outreach and recruiting strategies. These strategies apply data-mining algorithms to large databases created by combining numerous data sets from diverse sources. Organizations use these strategies to microtarget individuals who are more likely to join and fit well within their organizations; to help identify information that addresses their interests, needs, and questions; and to help choose the right places and times to provide that information to them in their decision process about joining the recruiter's organization.

While the military has had some success in applying these approaches, through the findings of this research, our sponsor sought to strengthen military recruiting by enabling the services and defense agencies and programs to more fully take advantage of new technological and methodological developments. To provide context for the information presented in this report, in this chapter we provide a brief discussion of key terms (*big data* and *AI*) relating to evidence-driven outreach and recruiting strategies, as well as of key concepts (*data-enabled business practices* and *successful implementation of data-enabled business practices*). It should be noted that, to date, researchers have not achieved consensus about how to define *big data* and related terms. The definitions presented here will likely change over time, but it is useful to capture how researchers understood such terms as a way of providing context for this study.

It should be noted that our description of these methods does not imply that we independently quantified their effectiveness or direct transferability to a military recruiting setting. Some of the methods we describe in this report are relatively new. Even though this is a very active area of research, knowledge about their effectiveness is still limited (see Chamorro-Premuzic, 2016; Akoka, Comyn-Wattiau, and Laoufi, 2017; Knight, 2017; Hutson, 2018; and Rahimi and Recht, 2017). Moreover, such assessments are well beyond the scope of this study, which focused on informing thinking about how the U.S. Department of Defense (DoD) and the services may be able to further deploy big data analytics in their outreach and recruiting processes. Our review of business and academic literature was not intended to suggest a one-to-one correspondence in potential outreach and recruiting practices, given differences in the demographics of the populations targeted, the characteristics required for entry, recruiting operations, and privacy policies governing outreach and recruiting for military versus civilian jobs.

Data-Enabled Business Practices

Organizations have traditionally used data and analytics to assist decisionmakers and evaluate the impact of decisions they made in the past to improve their performance (Davenport and Harris, 2017). Figure 1.1 illustrates key features of data-enabled business practices. An increasing number of organizations now use big data and analytics to *enable* employees to perform their tasks in the frontline operation—for example, to help marketers market and to help recruiters recruit. As the employees are performing their tasks, the organizations continue to collect new data from a variety of sources, including their employees; update the analytics; and deploy operational instructions to employees in near-real time.

Figure 1.1
Data-Enabled Business Practices

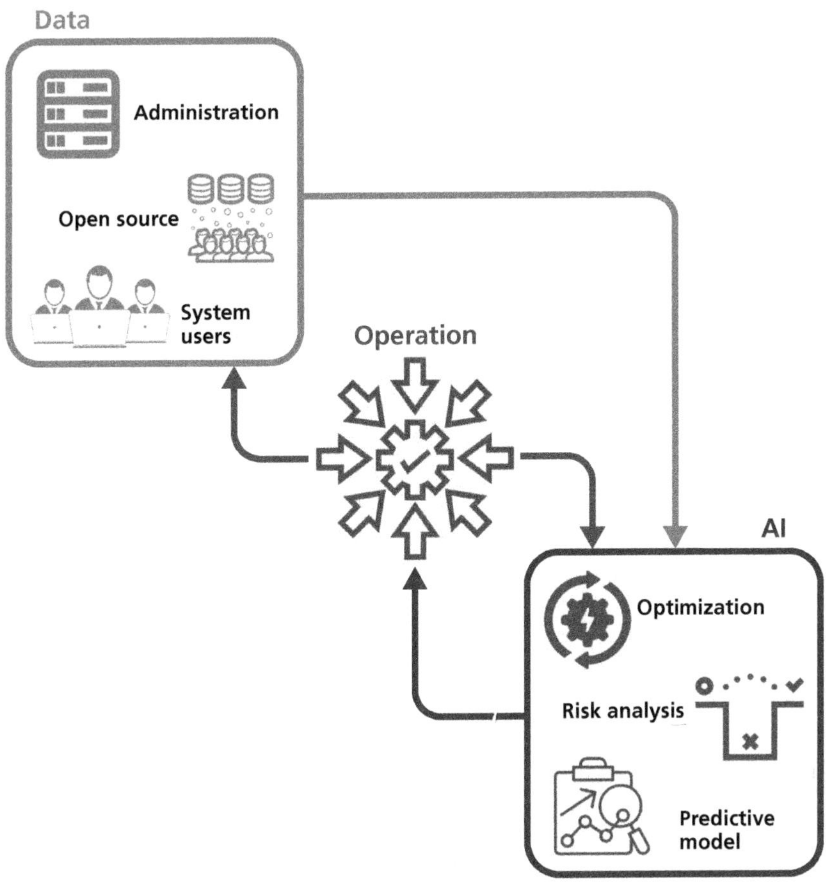

Big Data

As described by Ridgeway, 2017, *big data* "is a loose description for the general idea of integrating large data sets from multiple sources with the aim of delivering some new, useful insight from those data." Even though it is difficult to craft a comprehensive definition of *big data* (Davenport, 2014), big databases are unique in at least three dimensions:[1] Big data is massive in *volume*, and it comes with extremely high *velocity* from a *variety* of sources in numerous formats (Laney, 2001). For instance, McAfee and Brynjolfsson points out, "as of 2012, about 2.5 exabytes of data are created each day, and that number is doubling every 40 months or so. More data cross the Internet every second than were stored in the entire Internet just 20 years ago" (McAfee and Brynjolfsson, 2012, p. 3). The emerging databases are so large that the storage of these databases led to new and innovative technological developments, such as the Hadoop Distributed File System (Sharda, Delen, and Turban, 2018). Big data also represents databases that are collecting data at an unprecedented velocity and require management in near-real time. Finally, as more and more aspects of our daily lives are being digitized, data sources and their formats become numerous. Data can come from administrative databases collected by organizations, open-source data that are publicly available, and users of various systems. These data are stored in a variety of formats, from *structured*, numeric data in traditional databases to *unstructured* text documents, emails, videos, images posted to social media, audio, passive readings from sensors, and GPS signals from cellphones and satellites. The list of data sources and formats is continually expanding as new technologies are introduced.

Artificial Intelligence

Data alone cannot affect business strategies and practices. Data need to be transformed into business intelligence to enable frontline operations. An increasing number of organizations use AI to harness the transformational power of big data. *AI* is defined by Chui and McCarthy, 2018, "as the ability of a machine to perform cognitive functions we associate with human minds, such as perceiving, reasoning, learning, and problem solving." AI is made possible by advances in statistical learning processes called *machine learning*, "which are a collection of algorithms that detect patterns and learn how to make predictions and recommendations by processing data and experiences, rather than

[1] Saggi and Jain, 2018, identify seven V's of big data: volume, velocity, variety, valence, veracity, variability, and value.

by receiving explicit programming instruction. The algorithms also adapt in response to new data and experiences to improve efficacy over time" (Chui and McCarthy, 2018). The power of machine learning continues to increase as new analytical techniques are invented and computing capabilities continue to expand. For example, deep learning is a type of machine learning "that can process a wider range of data resources, requires less data preprocessing by humans, and can often produce more accurate results than traditional machine-learning approaches" (Chui and McCarthy, 2018). Deep learning models can ingest large amounts of data and build interconnected layers of a network that represent increasingly complex features of data at each layer. "The network can then make a determination [such as a prediction or classification] about the data, learn if its determination is correct, and use what it has learned to make determinations about new data" (Chui and McCarthy, 2018).

Using machine learning models, AI can help decisionmakers and frontline employees better *optimize* their operations, conduct *risk analysis*, and *predict* most possible outcomes of their actions. These analytical functions (optimization, risk analysis, prediction models) are not new. Organizations have used more-traditional analytical methods, such as operational research (e.g., Winston, 2003), econometrics (e.g., Wooldridge, 2010), and statistics (e.g., McClave and Sincich, 2012), to perform these functions for several decades. In fact, some machine learning methods use the same estimation procedures that traditional methods use. For example, regression methods, including ordinary least squares and logistic models; data reduction methods, such as principal component analysis; and classification models, including cluster analysis, are used in machine learning methods.

Machine learning differs from traditional methods in its usage of data, approach to the development of the models, and emphasis on prediction. As Mullainathan and Spiess, 2017, p. 87, points out, "machine learning not only provides new tools, it solves a different problem." Machine learning models iteratively uncover the underlying structure from the data and emphasize accuracy of predictions over estimation of causal inference between input variables and the outcome variable. By emphasizing the accuracy of the predictions, the machine learning models can provide decisionmakers with potential outcomes and tradeoffs among the options. However, machine learning models are not designed to address the potential impact of adding new input variables to the data set on the outcome variable. Comparing machine learning to econometrics, Mullainathan and Spiess, 2017, p. 88, wrote, "the success of machine learning at intelligence tasks is largely due to its ability to discover complex structure that was not specified in advance."

Successful Implementation of Data-Enabled Business Practices

The potential transformative power of data-enabled business practices through big data and AI is impressive and growing daily as new technologies and methods are introduced. However, advances in technical capabilities are necessary but not sufficient for successful implementation of data-enabled business practices. As Henke, Libarikian, and Wiseman, 2016, p. 2, reports, "an analytics-enabled transformation is as much about a cultural change as it is about parsing the data and putting in place advanced tools." The foundational determinants of successful implementation include data orientation, an appropriately skilled workforce, and IT infrastructure that can support the interconnected and interactive nature of big data and AI. In addition, a programmatic introduction to frontline employees is important in their adoption of data-enabled business practices. As we stated above, the effectiveness and feasibility of specific practices for an organization also should be considered.

Study Objective and Approach

While organizations outside DoD are reported to have benefited most from these changes, the military, too, has had some success in adopting data-enabled outreach and recruiting strategies. However, compared with private-sector organizations, many service and DoD leaders responsible for the oversight and conduct of military recruiting, including the sponsor of this research, perceive the progress to be slower. They view this as problematic because timely and targeted outreach to and recruitment of the required number of individuals with the desired characteristics is critical to a successful all-volunteer military force.

Through the findings of this research, our sponsor sought to better enable the services and defense agencies and programs, such as the Joint Advertising Market Research & Studies (JAMRS) program, to more fully take advantage of new technological and methodological developments.[2] Specifically, in concert with the sponsor, we agreed to address the following five research areas:

1. What are the services and JAMRS currently doing in their recruiting efforts, particularly in using data-enabled outreach and recruiting practices that might be adopted more widely?
2. How do organizations outside DoD use big data and analytics for recruiting?
3. What additional data-enabled outreach and recruiting practices do the services and DoD want to adopt to build on those they currently are using and to leverage approaches such as those used in the private sector?
4. What are the barriers to adopting such practices?
5. What actions could be taken to facilitate data-enabled outreach and recruitment in the services and DoD?

To address research area 1, the RAND National Defense Research Institute (NDRI) worked closely with the sponsor and services to identify and assemble an advisory group of representatives from the services' recruiting operations divisions, current marketing agencies, and JAMRS to share information on current strategies, policies, practices, databases, algorithms, and interactive tools being used in their outreach and recruiting efforts. Through the information provided in this forum, the purpose was to identify practices in which individual services and JAMRS were engaging that could be adopted more widely

---

[2] JAMRS does not conduct recruiting; it conducts research that the services use in their recruiting efforts and responsible government offices use in their recruiting oversight functions.

across the services, as well as to learn about issues or gaps in applying new technology and methods to support military recruiting. We also conducted focus groups with recruiters for the services to identify analogous strengths and issues at the local level.

As noted earlier, we reviewed business and academic literature describing the use of big data, machine learning, AI, microtargeting, applicant relationship management, and interactive tools and applications in marketing and recruiting. This literature review was intended to inform research area 2, by identifying strategies, policies, practices, databases, algorithms, and tools being used in outreach and recruiting efforts that might be applicable to military recruiting. The purpose was to inform thinking about how DoD and the services may be able to further deploy big data analytics in their outreach and recruiting processes, not, as noted, to suggest a one-to-one correspondence. There are differences in the demographics of the populations targeted, in the characteristics required for entry, in recruiting operations, and in privacy policies governing outreach and recruiting for military versus civilian jobs.

Last, RAND NDRI worked closely with the sponsor and services to identify and convene a meeting of key stakeholders, including legal, privacy, and policy experts and relevant DoD and service representatives, to discuss issues related to the DoD Privacy Program and use of new information and technology, including personally identifiable information (PII),[3] in military marketing outreach and recruiting, as well as their implications for DoD and service actions to modify the program to better capitalize on available information and technology for data mining and analytics. The results informed research areas 3 through 5. The results of the earlier tasks further informed these areas.[4]

---

3 The Office of Management and Budget (OMB) defines *PII* as "information that can be used to distinguish or trace an individual's identity, either alone or when combined with other information that is linked or linkable to a specific individual" (OMB, 2016a).

4 RAND's human subjects internal review board reviewed the research purpose and tasks. It determined that the "[p]lanned activity appears to fit the definition of DoD Instruction 3216.02 of not research involving human subjects: Activities, including program evaluation, customer satisfaction surveys, user surveys, outcome reviews, and other methods, designed solely to assess the performance of DoD programs where the results of the evaluation are only for the use of Government officials responsible for the operation or oversight of the program being evaluated and are not intended for generalized use beyond such program."

Organization of the Report

The structure of the report reflects the research areas requested by the sponsor and the resulting information. In Chapter Two, we begin by discussing what each service and JAMRS currently are doing in their recruiting efforts, particularly in using data-enabled outreach and recruiting practices that might be adopted more widely. This covers practices at both the national and local levels. In Chapter Three, we discuss data-enabled marketing and recruiting practices more generally, given their broader application outside DoD. Chapter Four covers additional data-enabled outreach and recruiting practices that the services and DoD want to adopt to build on their current practices and to more fully leverage data-enabled approaches, such as those used in the private sector. Chapter Five then discusses barriers to adopting such practices. Chapter Six briefly summarizes the additional desired data-enabled practices and the barriers to adopting them and then discusses implications for better realizing the benefits of data-enabled outreach and recruiting practices in the military, including actions that could be taken to address issues related to overcoming current barriers to doing so. Appendix A presents the interview protocol we used to conduct focus groups with military recruiters. Appendix B provides additional detail on the recruiting process.

CHAPTER TWO

Current Recruiting Practices in the Military Services

In Chapter One, we provided an overview of data-enabled marketing and recruiting using big data and AI. As noted earlier, RAND NDRI worked closely with the sponsor and services to identify an advisory group of representatives from the services' recruiting operations divisions, current marketing agencies, and JAMRS and to convene a meeting of the advisory group members to share information on current strategies, policies, practices, databases, algorithms, and interactive tools being used in their outreach and recruiting efforts, as well as challenges in applying new technology and methods to support military recruiting. The information was conveyed in a series of briefings given by attendees of the advisory group meeting. The goal was to learn and share information about what each service and JAMRS currently were doing in their recruiting efforts, particularly in using data-enabled outreach and recruiting practices that might be adopted more widely. We discuss outreach and recruiting operations below. The primary challenges reported in conducting these operations are discussed in Chapter Five. Table 2.1 shows the agencies represented in the advisory group.

Table 2.1
Members of the Advisory Group

Service or Organization	Agency
Army	U.S. Army Recruiting Command (USAREC) U.S. Army Cadet Command (USACC) Army National Guard (ARNG) Army Marketing and Research Group (AMRG) Headquarters, Department of the Army, G-1
Marine Corps	Active and Reserve
Navy	Active and Reserve
Air Force	Active Air Force Air Force Reserve Air National Guard (ANG)
Office of the Secretary of Defense (OSD)	Office of Accession Policy JAMRS
Institute for Defense Analyses (IDA)	

How the Military Services Currently Conduct Recruiting[1]

Operations

There is considerable consistency in marketing and recruiting activities across military services. The ultimate objective is to recruit the number of people required by the service in the given year, in the specific jobs that need to be filled, and with the specific physical and aptitude attributes that the service specifies for these jobs.

The services reported that they look at marketing at a broad national level, which focuses on awareness at a high level, and at more-specific and local levels, which is where recruiting operations

1 Although we provide an overview of military recruiting practices for readers less familiar with them than the primary audience for this research, it was not within the scope of this study to do a detailed review of the services' current outreach and recruiting practices or to assess their strengths and weaknesses. Rather, the purpose of this study task was to supplement routine interservice discussions by asking the services to provide examples of practices—in particular, data-enabled practices—that might be more broadly applicable in order to enhance awareness of emerging outreach and recruiting practices being employed in military recruiting across the services and OSD.

and individual recruiters operate. For example, the Army described its process in three stages. Awareness is the high level—the brand, the public's perceptions of the Army, whether a person knows anything about the Army or not, and so forth. The next level is engagement, which is where individual leads are gathered and validated. Leads come from the Army's major recruiting website (goarmy.com), phone lines, engagement with veterans, and a host of other face-to-face events and outreach efforts. At the activation level, recruiters begin to engage directly with prospective recruits—making and conducting appointments, leading to testing and contracts.

The recruiting process is often represented as a funnel. For example, in its briefing, the Air Force illustrated its recruiting funnel for the active enlisted force (Figure 2.1). The funnel concept is derived from the fact that the recruiting process starts at the top with a large number of leads, which produces a much smaller number of contracts at the bottom. For reasons along the way from the top to the bottom of the funnel, most leads fall out of the process. This can be due to a lack of interest, inability to meet physical requirements, criminal records, aptitude or education level issues, or other reasons.

As shown in the figure, at the beginning of the process, prospective recruits typically are prescreened for criminal records, age, and education. If prospective recruits pass that step, they can obtain an interview with a recruiter. During the interview, the recruiter gathers information on factors such as drug use, debt, tattoos, maturity, prospective aptitude test score (through a screening test), and other factors that may disqualify a prospect. If prospects make it past this point and remain interested, they are subsequently taken to a Military Entrance Processing Station (MEPS). There, prospects are aptitude tested and must achieve a minimum score on the Armed Forces Qualification Test (AFQT) to continue. Physical condition and history are then assessed as well. If an individual meets the basic aptitude and physical standards, he or she can then meet with a military job counselor at the MEPS. If interested in and qualified for the specific jobs that are available at that time, he or she can contract and be placed into the Delayed Entry Program (DEP), waiting to ship to basic military training (BMT). But, even at this stage, recruits can fall out of the funnel

Figure 2.1
Air Force Recruiting Funnel

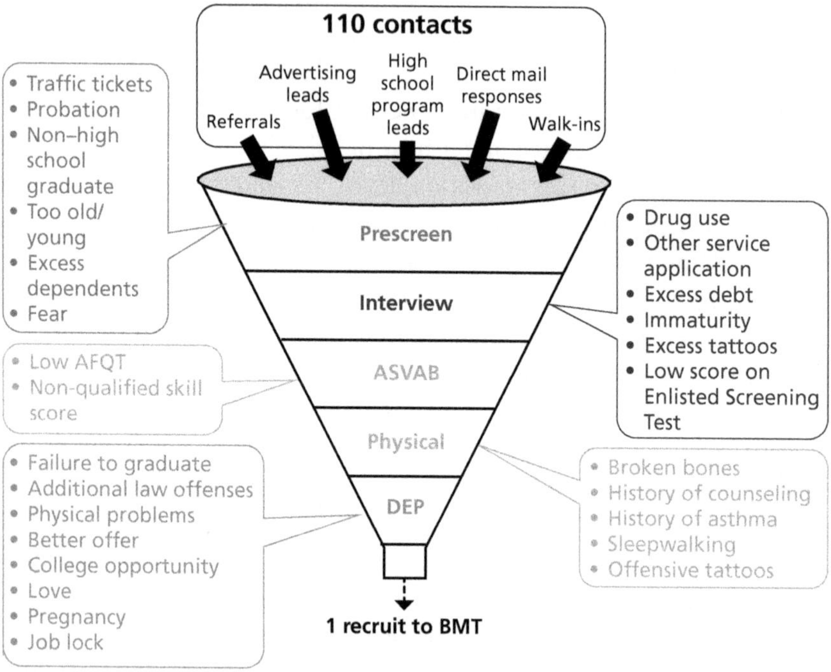

SOURCE: U.S. Air Force, 2018.
NOTES: ASVAB = Armed Services Vocational Aptitude Battery. Bubbles contain reasons for falling out of the funnel (i.e., the recruiting process).

for a variety of reasons. Such reasons include failure to graduate from high school, new physical problems or legal offenses, choosing to go to college or to work in lieu of serving, or other personal factors that draw them to other commitments. The rest enter BMT after formal accession into the service. As the figure shows, the Air Force reported that it takes 110 contacts—from referrals, advertising leads, high school program leads, direct marketing leads, and walk-ins—to get a single recruit under contract and into BMT.[2] While the contact-to-contract ratio can vary across services, the process that Figure 2.1 depicts is

2 The Air Force indicated that it does not routinely assign a loss value at each step of the funnel, in part because it varies depending on the geographic location and recruiter.

analogous across the services. Additional information on the process is provided in Appendix B.

Enlistment into the reserve components follows a similar set of steps and processes, though certain differences exist. For example, reservists enlist directly into units, not into the DEP, and are subsequently sent to training from their units. Reserve recruiting is more community-based and unit-centric. The reserves recruit in a more constrained geographic area, typically within 50–100 miles from the local reserve units. They recruit substantial numbers of individuals with prior military service, as well as individuals without prior military service, which creates two recruiting pools, whereas most recruits for active duty have no prior military service. The reserves also tend to recruit to fill a particular vacancy in a local reserve unit—a particular position in a specific geographic location. In the Air Force Reserve, for example, the Reserve Management Vacancy System identifies vacant positions; that information is used to develop plans to fill local positions. All services have such systems. The services also engage critical skills recruitment teams to focus on areas such as cyber, health, or other specialized skill areas.

Lead Generation, Data Collection, and Application

There also was broad commonality among the services in their accounts of how they generate leads (that is, information on or from people potentially interested in serving) and in the types of data that are collected in the recruiting process. All of the services reported that they combine primary data collection with third-party data to help target recruiting activities to the most promising areas. At the same time, it was clear from the activities reported in the individual service briefings that the level of detail at various stages in the recruiting process varies by service and stage, as anticipated in the purpose of the advisory group meeting to have the services share information on their ongoing data-enabled outreach and recruiting practices.

Leads are generated at the national and local levels. At the national level, leads can be generated through service websites (i.e., goarmy.com, navy.com, airforce.com); advertisements on TV, radio, and in print; educational tours, which offer students and influencers an overview of military careers on site; chat rooms; direct mail; call centers (1-800 numbers); mobile tours; and community activities, sports, or special events, such as air shows. Recruiters capture local leads via walk-ins, personal contacts, emails, telephone prospecting, local marketing events, public service announcements (PSAs), programs in high schools and community colleges, and other face-to-face encounters. One of the Army's practices in lead generation is through its Reserve Officers' Training Corps (ROTC) cadets, where the peer-to-peer interactions have been successful in identifying prospective recruits. The services' ROTC scholarship programs are also an important draw.

The services indicated that they collect only a limited amount of information from initial contacts—as little as name, address, and contact information (phone number or email address) and perhaps age and education level. This minimal information is sufficient for a recruiter to contact the individual. As an example, Figure 2.2 depicts the Air Force process for lead generation presented in connection with the DoD Privacy Program/PII workshop. The Air Force combines lead-related data from both the national and local levels based on information gleaned from the sources indicated. The combined data constitute prescreen information that gets entered into the Air Force Recruiting Information Support System–Total Force (AFRISS-TF). AFRISS-TF also collects information from users' interactions on www.airforce.com. In addition, recruiters enter information from the field using their mobile leads capture application. Additional information on the process is provided in Appendix B.

Recruiters obtain more-detailed information during an initial interview that assists the recruiter in assessing potential disqualification on factors such as age and education (if not collected earlier); finances; and medical, aptitude, and social issues. For example, the Air Force reported that its recruiters typically collect information during interviews on Social Security number, height, weight, place of birth, education, aptitude, medical history, law violations, drug usage, financial status, marital status, dependent information, citizenship, employment, driver's license, security information, tattoos, languages, religious preference, Selective Service number, and birth certificate. Such information contains a good deal of PII; current and potential expanded

Figure 2.2
Procedure for Providing Leads to the Air Force Recruiting Information Support System–Total Force

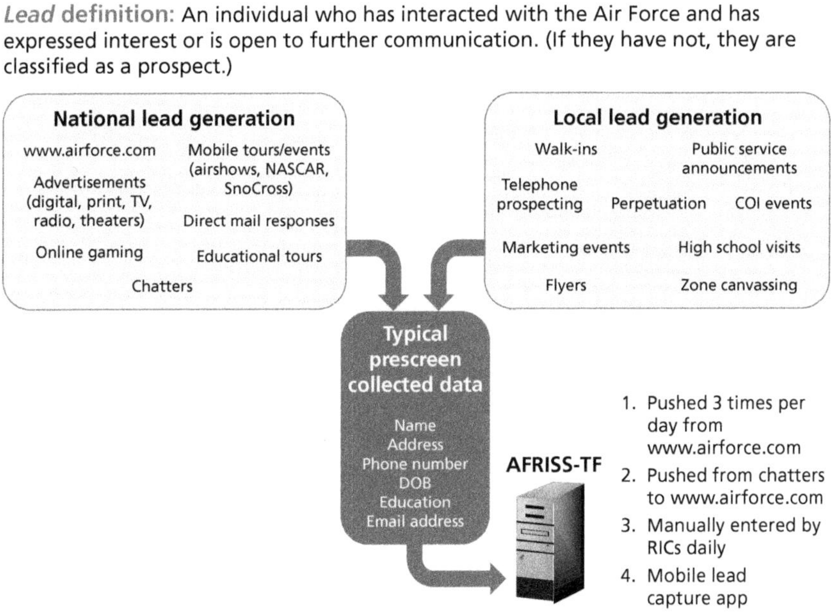

SOURCE: U.S. Air Force, 2018.
NOTES: Chatters are retired Air Force recruiters; COI = center of influence; DOB = date of birth; NASCAR = National Association for Stock Car Auto Racing; RIC = recruiter.

use of PII to support military recruiting is discussed in Chapters Four and Five. For potential recruits who proceed to the testing phases at the MEPS, data from the ASVAB and physical test results are added to a recruit's profile. The lead and subsequent information collected from potential recruits is submitted to one or more centralized databases within the services. Figure 2.3 illustrates the process used by the Air Force to enhance its lead data (which was shown in Figure 2.2). Additional information on the process is provided in Appendix B.

On the officer side, USACC indicated that it collects extensive information from prospects and recruits, similar to the other services. USACC uses the data to gather information on completion rates by different subgroups, including race/ethnicity, gender, and academic

Figure 2.3
Air Force Recruiting Lead Enhancement

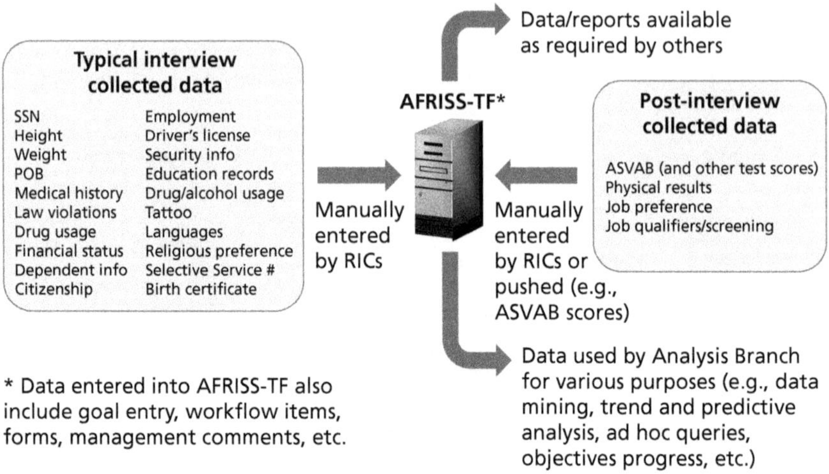

SOURCE: U.S. Air Force, 2018.
NOTES: POB = place of birth; SSN = Social Security number.

major, particularly science, technology, engineering, and mathematics (STEM) majors, among other uses. As part of its high school application, USACC also conducts a 95-question survey developed by the Army Research Institute. The survey is used to identify individuals with greater propensity to finish college and the ROTC program.

How the Services Currently Use Big Data and Analytics in Recruitment

Use of Third-Party Data

As discussed earlier, the more information that the services can collect and use, the better they are able to use data analytics to develop more-targeted and tailored outreach and recruiting strategies. The services reported that they supplement their own data collection about recruiting markets with information obtained from third-party sources. This information is used to construct target audience profiles; define the marketplace; and assess propensity to join, prior production, and receptiveness for specific markets. Data may be obtained to provide insights into demographics, psychographics, media consumption, the economy, population estimates, job markets, consumer trends, social attitudes, youth quality, and other similarly relevant factors. Sources to which the services reported turning include the Bureau of Labor Statistics, the Census Bureau, the Department of Education, the Defense Manpower Data Center (DMDC), the Internal Revenue Service, JAMRS, Pew Research, Kantar Millward Brown prospect/influencer attitudes, the Military Entrance Processing Command (part of OSD), the Director's Personnel Readiness Overview (Army), and others. For example, the Marine Corps spoke about how it targets direct mail, which it said is its top lead generator, using demographic data purchased from Acxiom combined with JAMRS data to target candidates with the highest propensity to enlist. The Acxiom data are appended to its prospect universe information for targeting purposes. The purchase and terms are reviewed by the legal team at J. Walter Thompson (the Marine Corps' advertising agency). The Marine Corps receives quarterly updates from Acxiom, and the new data replace the historical file. Historical Acxiom files are not retained or archived. Reserve components reported collecting forecasts of separations from the active component to use in developing a cross-component retention mission and, for those who separate from the active component without affiliating with a reserve unit, a marketing strategy targeted to prior-service recruits. Some of the services reported hiring private contractors to assist in market analysis.

One third-party source used extensively by the military services is DoD's JAMRS program. JAMRS provides market analysis that helps the services identify promising recruiting markets—pinpointing not only what markets have higher propensity but also why—as well as information on how best to engage with youth in those markets. JAMRS has extensive survey data from which it can analyze a particular market segment's lifestyle and media habits, as well as key drivers of propensity to join the military (e.g., attitudes, knowledge, self-efficacy, social norms). Combining geographic data and market segmentation in this manner provides the services with the means to tailor their messaging content and outreach efforts to each segment. JAMRS will identify the most-appropriate touch points (social media, phone, cold calling, email), motivations, and how to interpret them. JAMRS provides market segmentation analysis that identifies ZIP code concentrations of youth in high-accessing segments, the youth population eligible for service, high school seniors, college-enrolled youth, veterans, or other groups of interest. These analyses target youth markets most likely to join a particular service, to produce minority recruits, or to produce high-quality accessions. JAMRS also calculates a score that identifies which segments have been most productive for recruiting and provides the services with targeted recruiting recommendations down to individual ZIP codes.

An example involves the PRIZM Premier market segmentation tool. This information has been updated by JAMRS with service preferences, top motivators, and top barriers to enlistment that are prevalent within the youth and households in the segments. These allow for two tools highly relevant at the recruiting station: near-real-time measurement of the available Qualified Military Available population and the current penetration of that population by all of DoD.[3] It also provides microtargeted messages derived at the ZIP+4 geographic area, which can enhance recruiter engagements.

JAMRS provides a level of data standardization and useful derivations that are common to all services. According to a senior Army user, this is particularly useful when looking at historical enlistments and the DoD testing results. During the year, JAMRS has several interservice meetings at which it chairs discussions on advertising performance and on data standards and business rules. Data that are common for the services are collected and shared, for the most part, through the DMDC.

---

[3] The Qualified Military Available population is the number of youth eligible and available for enlisted military service without a waiver according to DoD. It represents the 17- to 24-year-old population after eliminating youth ineligible for service due to medical issues, weight, mental health, substance abuse, conduct, aptitude, or number of dependents.

How Personally Identifiable Information Is Currently Used

PII is used in many of the data-enabled recruiting practices we report below. While use of PII is limited in its extent at the early stage, an important use of limited PII is to help recruiters to generate leads for potential recruits. Once a lead has been identified, the next step is to enhance the information about that lead, which involves considerable additional use of PII. Drawing on first- and third-party data, the information is fleshed out, and the individual is categorized by recruiting subgroup. The enhanced leads are then scored and prioritized. The overall process involves constructing target audiences, prioritizing prospects, developing messaging strategies, and selecting tactics for outreach across a range of touch points. The process can include the use of cookies to develop profiles of the activity of those visiting service career sites, which enables more-targeted messaging to prospects that addresses their revealed interests and possible concerns. However, the development of the profiles cannot currently involve use of PII to track data across internet domains and data sources (see Chapter Five).

PII information also is used in analyses intended to refine a service's use of specific touch points—that is, various media that carry tailored messages to potential recruits or their influencers. They include television, websites, digital sources, direct marketing, social media, and experiential marketing, among others. The objective is to assess the effectiveness of the messages, whether they are properly delivered and placed, their outcomes, and how they can be optimally shaped. This includes assessing the best mix of marketing efforts and analyzing the operation and effectiveness of specific websites in reaching the intended target audiences and having the desired outcomes in favorably shaping attitudes toward the military and serving.

Promising Practices and Emerging Strategies Reported by Individual Services

At the individual service level, each of the services reported using data analytics to inform its outreach and recruiting activities to support the effectiveness and efficiency of its recruiting process. As discussed just above, the services use the data they collect to develop strategic recruiting plans and descriptive market assessments. The data are leveraged to develop messaging strategies, media strategies, and outreach locations and to provide insights for recruiters. The services use the data to assess how well they are meeting their annual goals and to provide insights on whether and how resources should be shifted to better attract recruits. The uses of data analytics reported by the services varied in the particulars, but the overall aim was to help recruiters achieve their mission—whether focused on locations, events, or individual prospects. Examples of how the services reported using data-enabled marketing and recruiting are listed below.

- The Air Force uses data analysis to construct target audiences that shape prospect prioritization, messaging strategies, and the selection of outreach tactics across touch points (e.g., television, websites, digital, direct marketing, social media, experiential marketing).
- The Air Force Reserve uses forecasts of separations to feed strategic planning activities. It examines markets and accession mix to inform advertisements for specific types of individuals.
- The Navy generates monthly production reports, creates trend and risk analysis, discerns relationships among data points, identifies gender differences, and develops recruiting predictive tools using a variety of statistical methods. Examples include aptitude predictors, DEP attrition analysis, a MEPS capacity and throughput model, officer and enlisted market segmentation, recruiter performance analytics, and cost projection planning (logistics, incentives). Production reports are being used both as descriptive summaries of historical data and, increasingly, for predictive and prescriptive reporting. The Navy reported using analytics to inform much of its recruiting decisionmaking. Examples include manpower allocation, resource allocation, and program and process improvements.
- The Marine Corps analyzes recruiting success at various stages of decisionmaking to obtain "health of the brand" measurements.
- USACC uses predictive analysis (the enrollment mission planner model) to determine what recruiting campaigns are required. The model is tailored to each school and market, historical trends,

and performance. The Army uses machine learning, cadet demographics, and surveys to examine past performance and to inform recruiting campaigns. It wants to extend this analysis to look at particular majors, such as STEM and nursing.

- AMRG uses analytic tools to select marketing venues—such as particular schools or competitions or the Super Bowl versus a baseball game—depending on its particular goals and also to determine where to purchase media and whom to target.
- USAREC uses analytics to inform the planning of recruiting activities and identify priorities. These analytics include lead refinement models, prospecting activity optimization, and classification of markets as "must win" and "must keep." This classification provides a level of prioritization that is applied to ZIP codes and schools at station level and is applied to larger markets up to the core-based statistical area at the company, battalion, and brigade levels. It aims to focus the recruiting effort on markets with the greatest potential for qualified, high-quality recruits. The command also uses analytics to determine resource allocation, mission assignment, targeting, and advertising campaigns to help maximize return on investment (ROI) and mission success.
- ARNG uses predictive modeling to generate mission estimates. It reported that among the most useful data analytic tools are the Director's Personnel Readiness Overview and the Recruitment Management Zone.

More generally, a number of the services reported using mapping applications that allow recruiters to visualize promising recruiting zones and location-specific trends. For example, the Graphical Accession Mapping and Analysis Tool can be used to identify enlistments, the prior service population, market potential by ZIP code, the college market, and trends. Mapping analytics can help identify where to focus recruiting efforts, depending on service goals. Some of the services reported using Google analytics to build maps for themselves.

The services reported that their use of social media is increasing and is perhaps becoming one of the most versatile tools at their disposal. The services use Facebook, Instagram, Snapchat, and Twitter.

Most of the services have developed social media presences at multiple levels—at the service level, this presence focuses on a national audience to build brand awareness and encourage military service; at the recruiter level, it focuses more on transactional messages, such as frequently asked questions and peer-to-peer conversations. Individual recruiters are able to build their own virtual networks, gain a following, and follow others, helping to create a sense of authenticity about military service.

The Army, for example, reported developing social media campaigns to personalize soldiers' experiences and allow potential recruits to see the Army at the individual level. In one campaign, individual soldiers shared their personal stories under a common hashtag, providing a single location at which individuals could gain insight from many perspectives into what it is like to be a service member.

Although a lot of the attention reported was focused on free social media outlets, paid social media brings an analytic dimension to the equation by enabling the services to examine how many people they have reached, key performance indicators, web traffic referrals, where visitors are coming from, who is sharing the services' content, and how. The Marine Corps talked about analyzing the social media patterns using multivariate analysis as an important part of making social media a force multiplier for recruitment.

The analytics and methods that the services reported using highlight several promising practices that could be expanded in the future. A capability that the Army reported in this regard is its Virtual Recruiting Center (VRC), which includes a Leads Refinement Center (LRC).

As leads are coming in, analytic models can be used to prioritize, clean up, and streamline those leads. The Army's LRC is an example of how such a system is currently being used to prequalify leads to confirm commitment and initial qualification to save recruiters' time. As shown in Figure 2.4, the LRC takes leads from a variety of sources, both paper and electronic. They include USAREC-generated leads and AMRG-generated leads. USAREC leads can come from local events, marketing, and advertising. They can be generated by Google event information or can be generated from student ASVAB tests, high school lists, goarmy.com visits, or virtual recruiting efforts. At the national level,

Figure 2.4
The Army's Leads Refinement Center

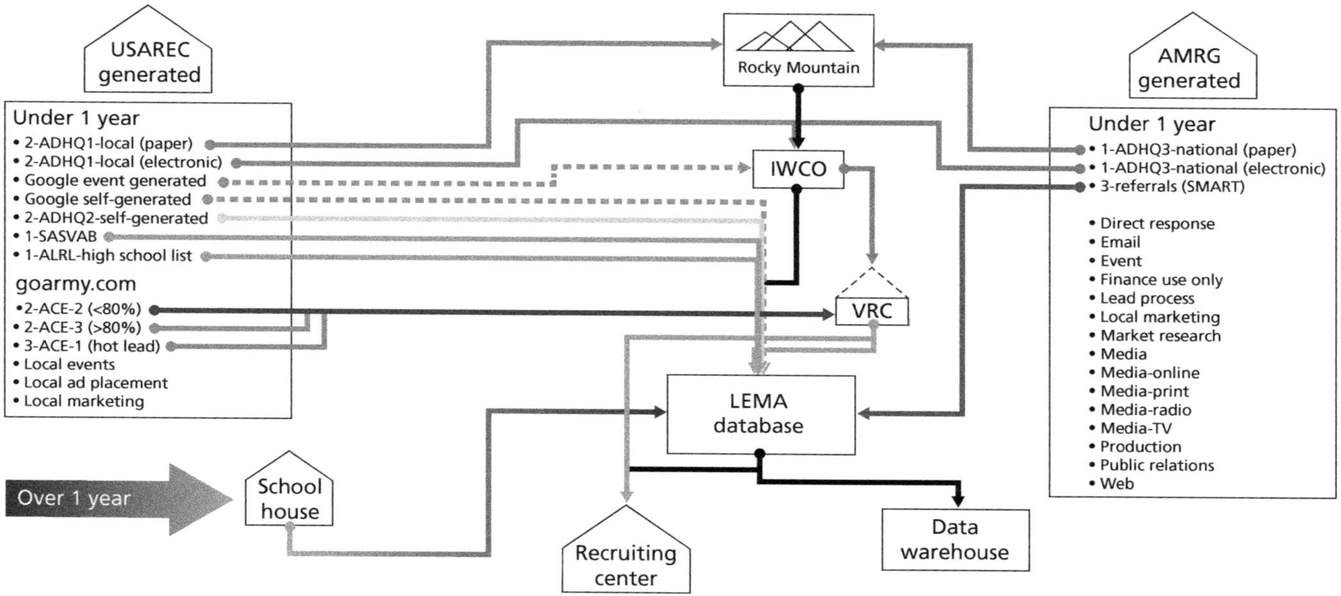

SOURCE: USAREC.
NOTES: ACE = Army Career Explorer (on www.goarmy.com); ADHQ = high-quality leads from advertising; ALRL = automated leads refinement list; IWCO is a direct marketing agency; LEMA = Leads, Mission, and Awards; SASVAB = leads from the Student ASVAB; SMART = Sergeant Major of the Army Recruiting Team.

AMRG-generated leads include direct mail responses; email; event-generated leads; print, radio, television, or online advertising; public relations campaigns; or other internet activities. Leads are fed into a centralized system. Every lead ends up as a record that is scored with a model. Recruiters then use the scoring to prioritize follow-up with leads. The leads scoring model can also use the data to examine a variety of outcomes—for example, the characteristics of individuals who ultimately sign a contract or the factors associated with reductions in recruit quality. The Army is working to refine the model to be more predictive of the full set of characteristics of the type of recruits it is looking for—recruits that are capable of meeting the "whole soldier" construct that captures cognitive, physical, and social requirements of training.

Within the Army, each agency entity is responsible for the verification and validation of models. Typically in USAREC, these are given oversight by the supervisor and collaboration within the work-group. The Army's manpower is insufficient to provide the level of peer review found in some other areas, according to the subject-matter experts (SMEs) providing the model oversight and review information. However, USAREC does participate in and presents at the Military Operations Research Symposium (MORS) and Army Operations Research Symposium when there are opportunities to share new advances, which often leads to interaction with the other services. Most recently at MORS, the SME indicated that there was good collaboration between the Navy and Army that continues today. The internal Army modeling efforts are relatively small efforts that are used for decision support and are adapted routinely based on commander guidance.

Our USAREC senior SME also indicated that the Army has identified a need for increased analytical expertise and the reconstitution of research and study support at the Training and Doctrine Command (TRADOC), USAREC, USACC, and subordinate brigade levels. To that end, additional analytical structure is being developed to improve the capability and process for model development, evaluation, and refinement. The TRADOC team is putting together more information under the TRADOC reform initiative for increasing analytical expertise.

The Army defines virtual recruiting as using digital methods to help find, influence, interview, qualify, process, and enlist or commission its future members. Virtual recruiting operations are carried out through digital systems using platforms such as email, the internet, and social media applications (e.g., Facebook, Twitter, LinkedIn, Snapchat). Virtual recruiting teams (VRTs) use only virtual recruiting processes to generate enlistments or commissions. Their activities include content creation and digital marketing analysis, supporting relationships with community partners, promoting and supporting Army events, and providing training and oversight to personnel in virtual prospecting, social media security, and regulatory compliance. The objective of the VRT is to generate additional, quality leads for the battalion. Lead refinement accounts for half of its activities and is focused on producing new and improved lead sources. Social media posting, prospecting, and lead generation make up the other half of the VRTs' activities.

In the recent past, USAREC has significantly expanded virtual recruiting, adding VRTs in each battalion and a "digital engagement fusion team" in the headquarters. VRTs initially generate, screen, and prioritize leads for stations; work to create social media interest before an event; train recruiters in the use of social media to initiate applicant processing, focus efforts on specific recruiting shortfalls, and work to increase interest in order to increase appointments; and conduct online interviews with recruits. Additionally, the capability requirements for the new Accessions Information Environment (AIE) include leads scoring and prioritization software built into the system and AI to help in that process. Also, USAREC is exploring pilot projects with industry that use AI "virtual bots" for data analysis and engagement strategies.[4]

More specifically, VRT operating procedures call for the station commander to oversee virtual lead generation, content creation, virtual marketing analysis, and market intelligence. This is done jointly with battalion "fusion and targeting cells." The station commander's responsibilities include collecting, analyzing, and reporting ROI for digital prospecting and marketing; training new virtual recruiters; assisting

4 Quotes in this paragraph and the two paragraphs that follow are taken from an SME's email.

in operational security management and regulatory compliance for social media efforts; ensuring content integration and synchronization between USAREC's website and social media platforms; promoting battalion-level events and community partner relations; "logistical coordination"; and virtual platform development and optimization.

VRT recruiters' responsibilities include lead generation and refinement; dissemination of leads and prospects to recruiting stations; content creation; social media security measures; support of virtual prospecting, digital media training, and community events; developing innovative virtual prospecting methods; information collection and reporting on the ROI of digital efforts (to the VRT station commander); researching "innovative tools, programs, systems, software, services and social media industry trends" to maintain current social media strategies; and adapting to digital media changes.

Recruiting stations' responsibilities include providing updates to the VRT weekly on the status of the leads provided to them. Leads are interviewed. When interviewing recruiters end processing for leads, they must provide the reason. This information supports analysis and refinement of the targeting process at higher echelons. Weekly in-process reviews (IPRs) are also held between the battalion VRT and companies. Contract credits for leads that continue forward to enlistment go to the station and recruiter, rather than to the VRT.

Figure 2.5 illustrates the VRC employed by USAREC at the time of the SME meeting, within which the LRC functions. The VRC is staffed with highly technical and analytical personnel. In addition to leads refinement and prioritization, the Army reported putting a lot of effort into virtual recruiting in the past two years to standardize recruiting efforts across its 38 recruiting battalions. The battalions work with virtual recruiters to plan activities, use telemining to resolve issues impeding enlistment among potential recruits, and search social media for individuals with interest in military service. As illustrated in the figure, the VRC capabilities can be conceptualized as falling into two groups: deliberate targeting and planned talent mining to fill specific needs and dynamic targeting to take advantage of targets of opportunity. For example, the Army described its success with virtual recruiting in filling shortfalls of military police in local reserve

Figure 2.5
Virtual Recruiting Efforts Employed by the U.S. Army Recruiting Command

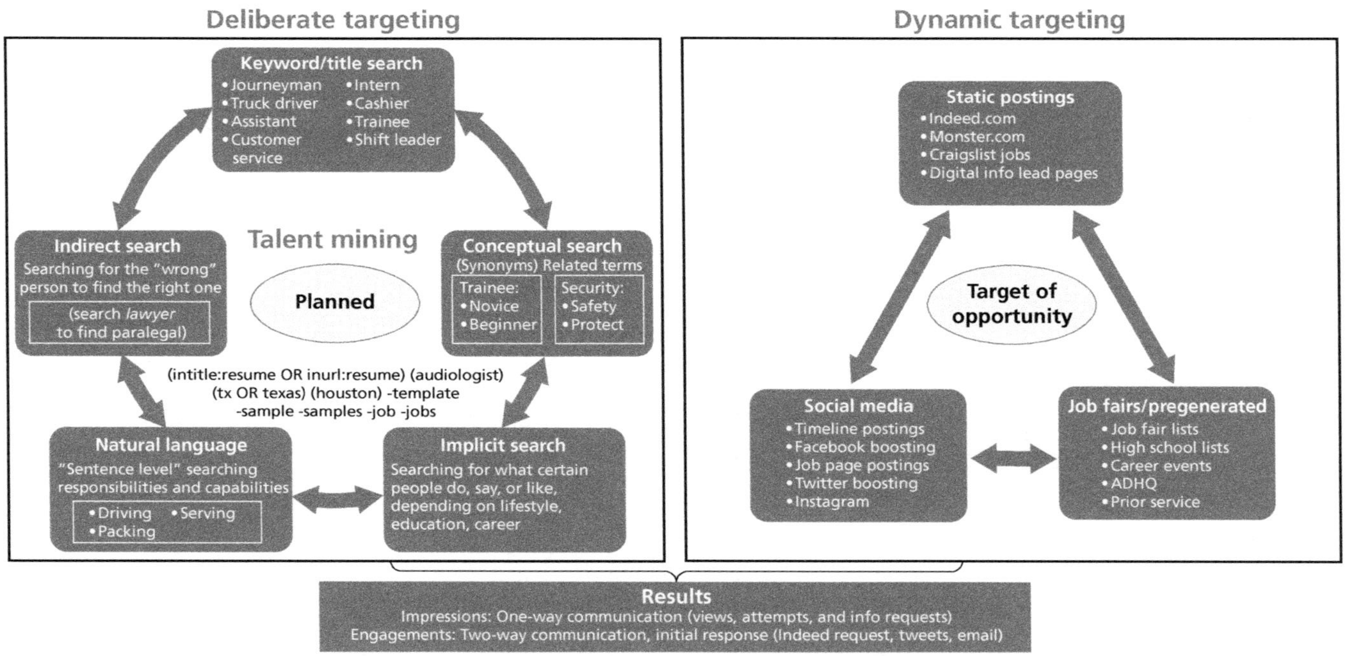

SOURCE: USAREC.
NOTE: ADHQ = high-quality leads from advertising.

component units. The VRC was able to target criminal justice majors at nearby colleges and universities with information about military police jobs and how involvement in such jobs could help them gain experience for their careers and money for their education. This led to success in filling these positions. This case illustrates how a small team with technical skills was able to focus on a particular need and target the right audience with the right information. This type of outreach would be difficult for individual recruiters in recruiting stations to carry out. Figure 2.5 provides examples of both types of recruiting targeting activities.

Virtual recruiting is not unique to the Army. The Navy also talked about the need to have a stronger virtual presence to supplement the force, given that recruiters cannot be in every ZIP code in every state. Making use of technology to better exploit social media tools is one aspect of virtual recruiting. The Navy has turned to the private sector to gather ideas on how larger corporations use data-enabled recruiting and how to expand its modeling efforts.

Recruiting at the Local Level

Above, we described information shared by our advisory group and DoD Privacy Program/PII workshop members on current strategies, policies, and data-enabled practices being used in service outreach and recruiting efforts. The SME group members operate on a national or command level. This section turns to those in the field who must carry out the recruiting mission locally. The services' ability to attract and recruit the personnel they need to carry out their missions depends in part on their frontline recruiters. As we have discussed, successful implementation of data-enabled recruiting involves providing important information and tools to recruiters, as well as recruiters' adoption of new technology and compliance with new policies and practices.

To better understand recruiting practices and challenges at the local level, we conducted focus groups with military recruiters across the services and components. As noted earlier, these focus groups were designed to supplement the SME information by providing perspectives and insights into the recruiting environment from those individuals directly executing the military recruiting mission at the local level. We sought to understand their current recruitment processes; the data analytics and tools currently used by recruiters and their effectiveness; and challenges or gaps associated with current policies, practices, data analytics, and tools. We begin this section by describing the methodology used to conduct this qualitative analysis. The resulting findings concerning local recruiting practices follow. Challenges at the national, command, and local levels are discussed in Chapter Five.

Methodology for Focus Groups

RAND team members conducted ten focus groups across all four services, including representation from active-duty and reserve component recruiters, primarily in the broader Los Angeles and Washington, D.C., metropolitan areas. RAND personnel worked with advisory group members from each component to identify local recruiting offices in these areas for participation. Recruiters represented urban, suburban, and rural environments. Table 2.2 shows the range of recruiting environments across the service components included in the focus group

Table 2.2
Focus Group Components and Recruiting Environments

Component	Urban	Suburban	Rural
Army	X	X	
Marine Corps		X	X
Navy	X	X	
Air Force	X	X	X
Air Force Reserve	X	X	X
ARNG	X	X	X
ANG	X	X	X

NOTES: The Air Force Reserve is a separate recruiting command for the Air Force. Reserve recruiting is included with active-duty recruiting for the other military services.
National Guard recruiting is separate for both the Army and Air Force.

sample. Note that each focus group included recruiters from one military service and from one recruiting area, typically representing various recruiting environments in the geographic area.[5] Because the services typically recruit for both active-duty service and the reserves, recruiting strategies for both populations were discussed in the same focus group. The exception was the Air Force, where the active-duty Air Force and Air Force Reserve are separate recruiting entities; therefore, separate focus groups were held for each. For analogous reasons, separate focus groups were held for ARNG and ANG. We recognize that not every environment was covered for each service component. However, we heard common themes across groups, and, after the tenth group, we believed that we were reaching a saturation point and that adding additional focus groups was unlikely to materially alter the findings.

We asked participating recruiting offices for roughly five to eight recruiters for each focus group. While most focus group sizes fell within this range, some focus groups included slightly fewer participants when based in smaller recruiting offices. Focus group discussions ran for approximately 60 to 90 minutes.

RAND focus group facilitators began each session by providing background information on the study and administering informed consent. This process included emphasizing the amount of time required, explaining the voluntary nature of participation, and assuring participants that comments provided would be kept confidential by the RAND research team and not reported in a manner that would be identifiable. A notetaker from RAND also attended each focus group session; this person took transcript-style notes of the discussion without including participant names or any other identifiable information in the notes. See Appendix A for the protocol questions used to guide focus group discussions. Once all focus groups were completed, the RAND research team analyzed the detailed focus group notes using qualitative data coding techniques. Our coding analysis used both deductive and inductive methods: Deductive methods were driven by the protocol question areas, and inductive methods were used to

---

5 Geographic areas can cover distances of more than one hour of driving time.

explore the qualitative data and code as themes emerged organically across focus groups.

Focus Group Results

Key results from the recruiter focus groups emerged in three main areas: (1) current recruiting practices, (2) IT infrastructure, and (3) analytical tools. We discuss current practices below; IT infrastructure and analytical tool issues are discussed in Chapter Five.

In general, the recruiters indicated that they developed or adapted their own recruiting strategies aimed to most effectively recruit in their assigned area. Strategies are often passed down at the local level as new recruiters come on board at a specific recruiting office. For example, many recruiters noted using a preset list of questions when engaging with high school students in the classroom. Recruiters also described developing or adapting their own questions that they deemed would most effectively gauge student interest or propensity to serve and also assess, at a general level, students' ability to qualify for military service. When asked if such questions were standardized across the service, a recruiter from one focus group responded,

> Everyone does something different. I made three different versions I can use. You have to tailor it to your audience.

Recruiters described passing ideas for questions to one another in their recruiting offices and passing these down to new recruiters who were assigned to the same area.

When recruiters discussed differences regarding their target population and adjusting strategies accordingly, some recruiters described these differences as being driven by whether an environment was urban, suburban, or rural. One recruiter noted,

> For me, I'm in a more rural area that's 1,400 square miles. So, I try to reach them [potential recruits] at schools or via phone calls. But when I go to a more suburban area, I go to the mall and run into kids there.

However, most recruiters reported that the recruiting strategies they opt to employ are driven more by socioeconomic factors and attitudes toward the military in an area rather than the geographic environment. Socioeconomic factors impact potential recruits' interest in and reasons for or against joining the military, affecting the approach that recruiters will take to be most effective. For example, recruiters noted that money for college as a military service benefit is typically more attractive in poorer areas, where opportunities for education are more limited than in wealthier areas.

> If it's a more well-off area instead of talking about "money for school," it's more "your adventure" or sometimes it's "serving your country." And in poorer areas, you are talking about the signing bonus or money for school—so it varies by the customer.

Attitudes toward the military and how friendly an area's population is to military members also were reported to affect the approaches that recruiters can use to recruit effectively and may limit certain avenues for access to potential recruits. For example, if schools in a certain area do not have a positive attitude about the military, they can make it difficult for a recruiter to gain the access and student information that is required by law. JAMRS published a white paper in June 2017, *Barriers to Recruiter Access in High Schools*, after meeting with and surveying recruiters. In the conclusion, JAMRS noted, "Accessing high school students and student directories can be challenging for recruiters, despite laws that require schools to provide access. While half of the respondents say that they were satisfied with the cooperation they got from their assigned high schools, they repeatedly mention that while they are allowed access, the quality of the interactions that were being allowed by schools was hampering their efforts to recruit effectively. This suggests that the recruiting force feels that schools are meeting the letter, but not necessarily the spirit, of the law. Additional work in this area is needed to see if there are policy changes that can improve this barrier" (JAMRS, 2017).

Prioritization

Focus group participants discussed methods for prioritizing recruiting leads (i.e., prospective recruits), as well as recruiting activities. When asked about strategies or tools used to prioritize recruiting leads, recruiters described that this is primarily conducted in an ad hoc manner, not in a standardized way or by using advanced tools. Recruiters typically prioritized leads according to any initial screening or background factors that help them to determine interest and qualification. For example, if a recruiter has a good conversation with a potential recruit at an event and he or she indicates a high level of interest in military service and looks physically fit, the recruiter may fold the corner of the contact card to indicate a higher-priority lead. Similarly, if a recruiter is in a high school classroom and collects information from students, the recruiter may rank the priority level of those responses and determine follow-up priority based on that information. One participant explained this process as follows.

> You get leads from classroom questions and I [rank them]. So, if he is overweight, I put a negative sign. And if he looks good, I'll put a star or a 10. If I put down a 1, I won't waste my time following up.

Recruiters reported that they largely prioritized which schools to engage with most frequently based on past success of recruiting students from the schools, as well as on the relationships with the schools and how friendly they are to the military. Many recruiters described ranking systems for schools of priority 1, 2, or 3, which dictates the frequency of visits. One participant described how those decisions could be made.

> If the counselors and the faculty are friendly to us, then this school is open to us. They'll say, "Hey, I have this class where you can do a presentation." We prioritize those schools because the more kids we talk to in a school, the higher percentage that one of those kids will sign up with us.

Recruiters reported that sometimes these priority rankings are passed down to them but that they often have the ability to adjust priority rankings at the local level to some degree.

Recruiters also reported that recruiting events they were expected to attend were often prioritized in an ad hoc manner. Many stated that they did not believe that the ROI was maximized to prioritize the highest-return events. One participant mentioned a specific event that he felt was not prioritized correctly.

> We had a booth at the [football] game that cost a lot. People were just coming up to us for free stuff. I walked away with no leads. It was a total waste.

CHAPTER THREE

Data-Enabled Marketing and Recruiting in Non–U.S. Department of Defense Organizations

As is true for military service recruiters, the overarching goal for recruiters outside DoD is to fill required positions in their organizations with qualified people. To accomplish this goal, recruiters need good leads, to convert those leads into applicants, and, finally, to convince the best applicants who can do the job and will fit in well with the organization to take the job offer. This chapter describes how marketers and recruiters approach this goal through the use of big data and AI in settings outside DoD, such as the private sector. We address two specific questions: (1) How are data-enabled marketing and recruiting practices being used by these organizations? and (2) What are determinants of successful implementation of such practices?

To address these questions, we used a mixed-methods approach. We sought relevant publications that represent the intersection of multiple subjects: big data, machine learning, deep learning, AI, marketing, recruiting, and human resources (HR) practices. We conducted a series of searches in publication databases such as Academic Search Complete, Business Source Complete, Scopus, Social Sciences Abstracts, and Web of Science with a set of inclusive search terms.[1] In

1 For example, to identify peer-reviewed journal articles, we used this search string: (employee* OR workforce OR "work force" OR personnel OR talent) AND (recruit* OR select* OR screen* OR marketing OR advertising OR branding OR hiring) AND ("data analytics" OR "business analytics" OR digitiz* OR software OR "social media" OR "big data" OR method* OR technique* OR platform* OR "candidate relationship management" OR algorithm* OR "machine learning" OR "artificial intelligence" OR "data mining").

addition, we conducted citation analysis using Google Scholar. After we had identified a set of useful publications, we used targeted citation searches using the "cited by" function of Scopus and Web of Science to review additional documents that cited these key publications.[2] We found that the academic research on the use of machine learning, deep learning, and AI in marketing and recruiting is limited. Most of the articles we identified through searches did not directly address our topics. The articles mainly dealt with conceptual and methodological issues associated with various aspects of data, techniques, and ethical issues. They did not holistically describe or evaluate how organizations in the private sector use data-enabled methodologies in marketing and recruiting or their effectiveness.

In addition to reviewing published documents, we reached out to organizations that provide data-enabled marketing and recruiting services. Not surprisingly, we found very few organizations that were willing to share their business practices for publication, even though there are a variety of informal sources—including blogs, YouTube interviews, and presentations—discussing the use of data-enabled practices at large companies, such as Amazon, FedEx, and McDonalds.[3] Fortunately, we were able to conduct structured discussions with representatives from Salesforce. In addition, we conducted a discussion with J. Walter Thompson, the marketing agency for the U.S. Marine Corps, and received a formal briefing from Mullen Lowe, a marketing agency associated with JAMRS and OSD. Marketing agencies working with the services, including J. Walter Thompson and Mullen Lowe, attended our meetings and shared their insights. These marketing agencies provide data-enabled marketing and recruiting services to their private-sector clients.

---

2 In this process, we reviewed more than 300 articles. We found a large number of publications in popular and business publications about the use of big data and AI in HR practices, including recruiting and selection. We found relatively fewer peer-reviewed journal articles (20) on the same subjects. We found additional peer-reviewed journal articles (50) by browsing targeted journals and magazines.

3 Smashfly Technologies, 2017; Bersin, 2017; Inside Amazon Videos, 2017; Indeed.com, 2015; Mayer, 2015; Indeed.com Blog,2016; and Strazzulla, 2017.

As discussed in Chapter Two, the military has had some success in adopting data-enabled outreach and recruiting strategies. However, as also noted, DoD senior leaders consider its progress to be slower than in outside organizations. The information documented in this chapter is intended to inform thinking about how DoD and the services may be able to further deploy big data analytics in their outreach and recruiting processes. Given differences in the demographics of the populations targeted, the characteristics required for entry, recruiting operations, and privacy policies governing outreach and recruiting for military versus civilian jobs (see Chapter Five), we are not suggesting a one-to-one correspondence.

Data-Enabled Marketing: Using Big Data and Artificial Intelligence to Generate Good Leads

Big data and AI have potential applications in all stages of marketing and recruiting practices. Figure 3.1 illustrates the first stage of a data-enabled recruiting process:[4] data-enabled marketing that converts potential applicants into good leads for recruiters. The illustration is based on our discussion with representatives from Salesforce (2017a), J. Walter Thompson, and Mullen Lowe and our review of the literature on data-enabled marketing.

The foundation of the process is big data that continually gathers information about potential applicants by capturing data from a wide variety of sources. The assembled big data enables marketers to build profiles and unify the information of potential applicants in near-real time. Next, using AI, marketers analyze potential applicants' information and assess their preferences and propensity to join the organization at the micro (individuals and population segments) and macro (nation and regions) levels. Based on the analytical results, marketers design and execute targeted marketing campaigns with the goal of optimizing them to resonate with potential applicants. This data-enabled

---

[4] We adopted a framework from Artun and Levin, 2015, to describe the data-enabled marketing approach for recruiting purposes.

Figure 3.1
Structure of Data-Enabled Marketing Process

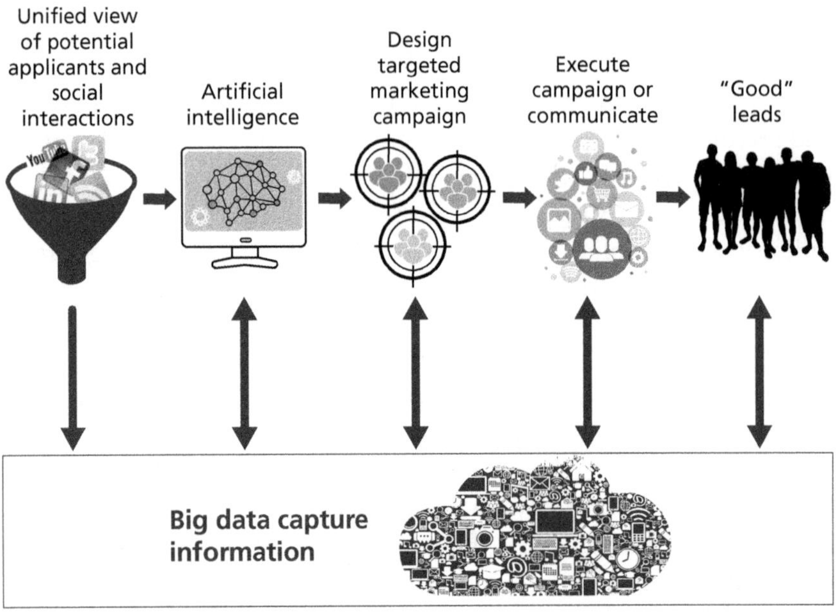

marketing is designed to convert potential applicants into good leads by providing potential applicants personalized experiences across all touch points (e.g., social media, phone, email) in the marketing process.

Content of Big Data

The information that marketers can gather about potential applicants to assemble a big data source is impressively comprehensive. For example, Mullen Lowe reported a sample of the data that are available for marketers at one of our meetings with key stakeholders (Table 3.1).

As shown in Table 3.1, true to the nature of big data, marketers often gather information about individuals from a variety of sources. Marketers have access to personal information, (e.g., race/ethnicity, occupation, education, religion, salary/income, home ownership, voting records, and party registration); health status (e.g., allergies, diets, and addictions); life event triggers, including changes in marital status (getting married, getting divorced), making key purchases

Table 3.1
A Sample of Available Data

Data Category	Data Examples
Biographical	• Name • Address • City • State • ZIP • Age • Race/ethnicity • Occupation • Education level
Life event triggers	• Getting married • Buying a home • Sending kids to college • Graduation • Getting divorced • Pregnancy • Pet adoption
Charitable giving	• PBS • Animal welfare • Child welfare
Hobbies	• Likes to golf • Likes to run • Type of novels read • Cooks
Purchases made	• Retail • Travel • Restaurants – Online/offline
Personal/finance	• Religion • Detailed salary and pay stub information (38 percent of working Americans) • Home ownership – Size of home – Purchase price – Amount owed
Government records	• DMVs: type of vehicle owned • Public voting records – Party registration

Table 3.1—Continued

Data Category	Data Examples
Health	• Allergy sufferers • Dieters • Online search propensity – Ailments and prescriptions – Family medical history – Cancer – Heart disease – Purchase plus-size clothing
Internet	• Cookies • Search engine history • Email • Retail and content websites • Social networking services • Blogging
Social media profile	• Screen name • Website addresses • Interests • Hometown • Professional history • Number of friends/followers
Specialized lists	• Addictions – Paramount – Alcohol – Sexual – Gambling

SOURCE: Mullen Lowe and Office of People Analytics.
NOTES: DMVs = Departments of Motor Vehicles; PBS = Public Broadcasting Service.

(buying a home), life-cycle changes (pregnant, sending kids to college); and major purchases (e.g., retail, travel, and restaurants). In addition, marketers can gather behavioral information about potential applicants, such as charitable giving, hobbies, internet searches, and social media profiles.

Application of Artificial Intelligence in Marketing

To help microtarget potential applicants more effectively, marketers can apply AI to big data to create behavioral and psychological profiles of potential recruits, predict their preferences, and gauge the propensity of potential applicants to join an organization. (See Figure 3.2.)

Figure 3.2
An Illustration of Market Segmentation and Microtargeting

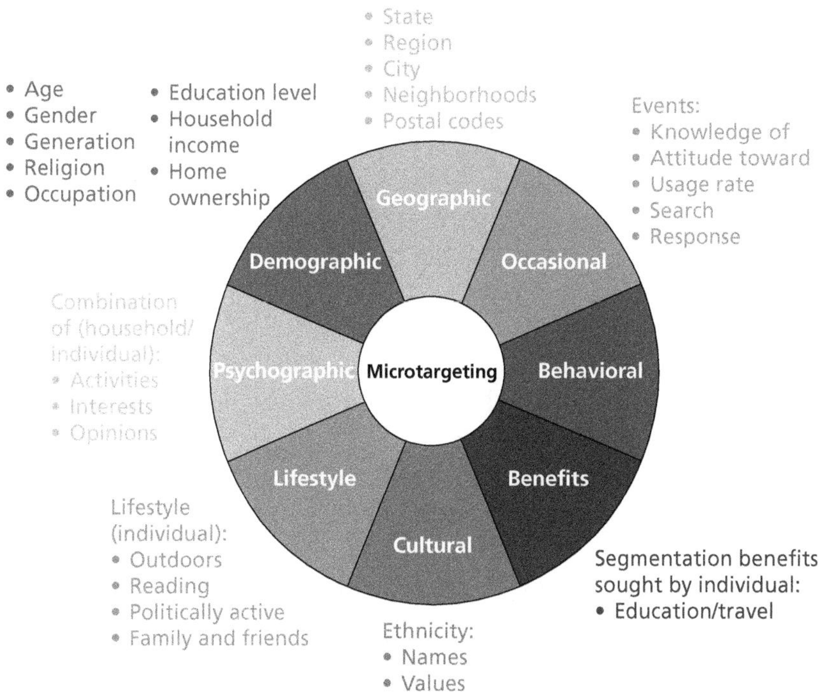

SOURCE: Mullen Lowe and Office of People Analytics.

The AI methods that marketers use can be grouped into three categories (Artun and Levin, 2015):

1. **Clustering methods to identify population segments.** The clustering algorithms, such as k-means and a priori algorithms, are known in the literature as *unsupervised learning* models because these models do not have specific outcome variables. Instead, the models identify population segments that contain individuals who have similar backgrounds, preferences, and behaviors. Marketers can use the results from these clustering methods to design and execute personalized marketing campaigns and provide a personalized experience for potential applicants.

2. **Predictive models to estimate preferences and the propensity of potential applicants to join an organization to prioritize the recruiting effort.** These models are known as *supervised learning* models because the models are designed to predict specific outcomes or behaviors of potential applicants. For example, an AI model can predict the likelihood of a positive reaction from a potential applicant to particular marketing messages. The latest machine learning models, including deep learning, iteratively discover the complex structure of underlying data to make the models' predictions as accurate as possible. These predictive models construct layers of networks that can capture direct and interactive influences of predictors (or factors) on the outcome. It is important to note that these models are designed to be applied to future data by not "overfitting" the historical (or training) data.
3. **Reinforcement learning methods to assist potential applicants based on their behavioral responses to marketing campaigns.** Unlike clustering and predictive methods, reinforcement learning methods help marketers predict the best next steps, outcomes, content, or events for applicants by applying "a trial-and-error-based learning scheme" (Artun and Levin, 2015, p. 25).

The extent of the impact of AI on frontline operations depends on several factors, including the richness of the data assembled, the accuracy of analytical results, and the interactivity between the AI and the frontline marketers. For the system to improve its effectiveness over time, it must be able to learn from the experience of the users of the system. Without this feedback, the system cannot be considered a learning system.

Data-Enabled Recruiting of Good Leads

Data-enabled recruiting starts where the marketing process ends: good leads. As we stated above, the primary goal of the recruiting step is to convert good leads into applicants and persuade the best applicants to take the job offer. As in marketing, developments in big data, machine learning, and technology have transformed how companies identify, engage, monitor, and track potential applicants in the private sector (Maurer, 2015; Roepe, 2017; Berkelaar, 2017). The applications of data and analytics for marketing and recruiting are similar, but the operational emphasis and details are different. The operational emphasis of data-enabled recruiting is to provide an integrated process to potential applicants and to manage available resources effectively and efficiently. For many companies, an integrated strategy is now an important part of candidate identification and initial contact. As part of this strategy, technology in recruiting, hiring (job offer), and onboarding is applied end to end, at all phases. An integrated customer relationship management (CRM) platform provides such integration and is facilitated through a cloud-based, stable IT infrastructure. Figure 3.3 shows a data-enabled recruiting process. The figure is based on our discussion with representatives from Salesforce and review of the literature.

As with generating good leads through data-enabled marketing in the previous step, the recruiting step begins by gathering information about good leads from a variety of sources. This information can

Figure 3.3
A Data-Enabled Recruiting Process

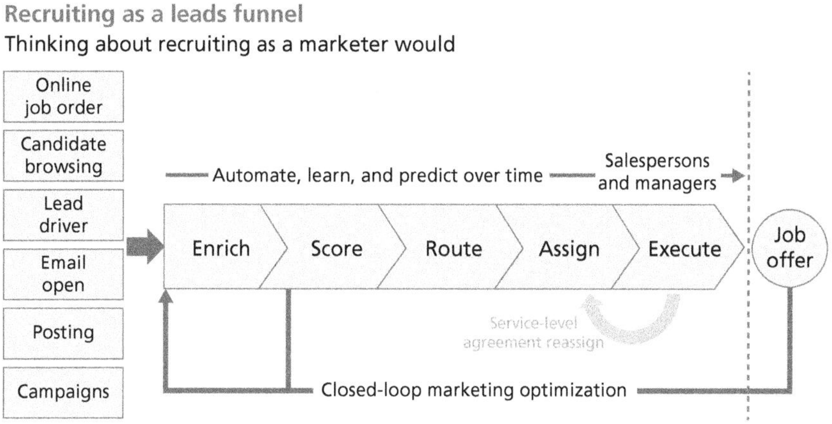

SOURCE: Salesforce, 2017b.

include leads' behaviors in responding to marketing campaigns, job postings, emails, and online activities. Next, the recruiting organization *enriches* the data by combining them with additional data that the organization can acquire from other organizations (data brokers, such as Acxiom, LexisNexis, Experian, Equifax, and TransUnion). The recruiting organization then develops AI models that *score* the leads based on the probability of accepting the job offer if it is given and the suitability of the leads for employment in the organization. In this step, the recruiting organization uses longitudinal data of past leads and current employees of the organization, including their personal profiles and job performance. Based on their estimated scores, the leads are then assigned to recruiters that the organization perceives to be most likely to be able to establish a good rapport with the leads. In the final step, recruiters execute the process to try to convince the best applicants to accept the job offer.

Throughout the outreach and recruiting processes, marketers and recruiters provide personalized experiences using CRM systems. (See Figure 3.4.) CRM is designed to manage and strengthen relationships with potential and current job applicants. The technology is used to automate communication with these people, encourage engagement, and improve their experience—for example, by creating email campaigns providing targeted content and by ensuring that their experience and support is consistent with the SLA.[5]

Determinants of Successful Implementation of Data-Enabled Marketing and Recruiting Practices

Successful implementation of data-enabled marketing and recruiting practices can help to target resource allocations based on strategic objectives and likelihood of success, as well as assist in the personalized management of applicants. The *potential* power of these practices

[5] For CRM services provided to the military, an SLA would function similarly to one outside DoD. If owned by a military service, it would equate to ensuring that the level of information and support provided is sufficient to meet a potential enlistee's information needs and timeline for receiving information and remaining engaged in the enlistment process.

Figure 3.4
Illustration of a User Interface from the Salesforce Customer Relationship Management Program

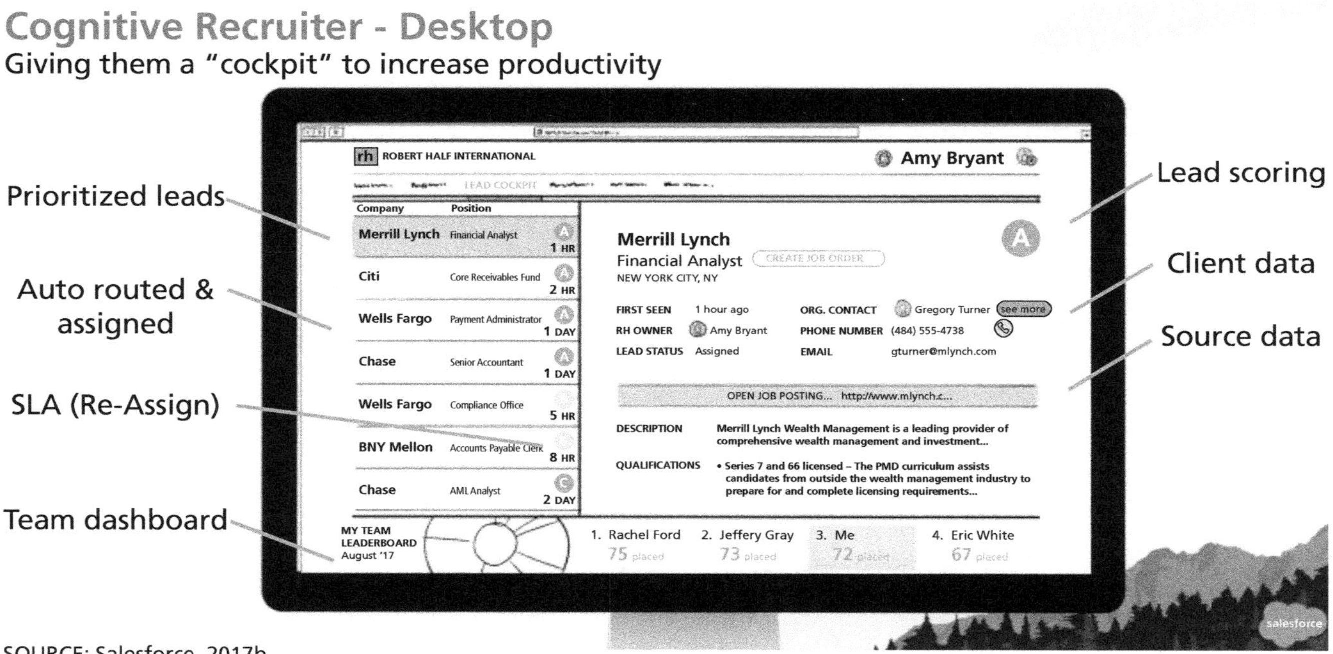

SOURCE: Salesforce, 2017b.
NOTE: SLA = service-level agreement.

appears impressive, and their sophistication increases as new technologies and methods are developed. At the same time, understanding of the effectiveness and the applicability of these techniques in a variety of organizational settings is limited (Gunter et al., 2017; Sivarajah et al., 2017). As Gunter et al., 2017, p. 192, stated, "high hopes and extensive publicity regarding big data do not guarantee the gaining of actual value, and may lead organizations to believe they can gain more value from big data than they are actually able to realize in practice." For example, we do not know how data-enabled marketing and recruiting practices impact the quality and characteristics of new recruits. Chamorro-Premuzic et al., 2016, states, "there is little scientific research on innovative assessment methods, leaving HR practitioners with no credible evidence to evaluate the utility of such tools."

There are significant challenges in implementation of a big data strategy across different stages of the data life cycle, as depicted in Figure 3.5 (Sivarajah et al., 2017, p. 265). First, the characteristics of big data (volume, velocity, variety, variability, veracity, visualization,

Figure 3.5
Conceptual Classification of Big Data Challenges

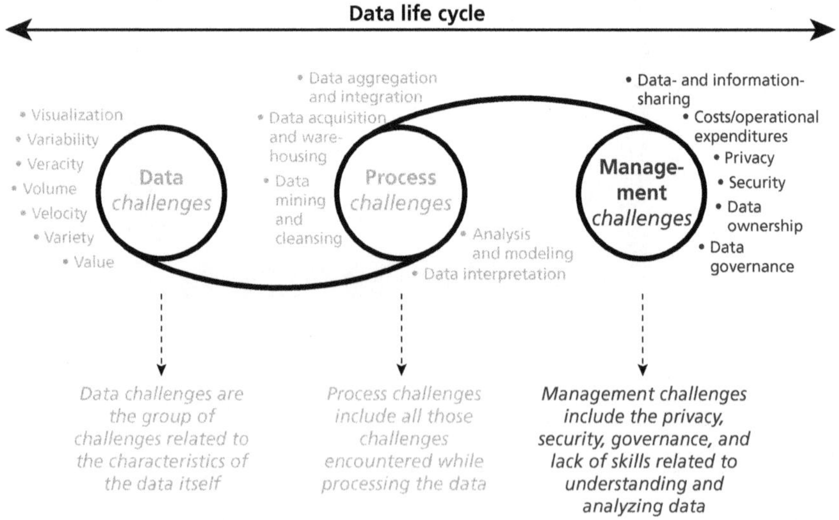

SOURCE: Sivarajah et al., 2017.

and value) pose significant challenges. Next, how an organization processes big data to transform the *raw* data into business intelligence poses challenges. The IT infrastructure needed to collect and maintain big data can be costly, even with the availability of cloud computing technologies. In addition, the sheer size and complexity of big data pose challenges to existing analytical techniques (Marjani et al., 2017; L'Heureux et al., 2017). Finally, even if an organization has successfully overcome data challenges and process challenges, the organization faces management challenges that include concerns for privacy, security, data governance, information-sharing, resources, and ownership of the data.

Based on our literature review and discussions with SMEs, we conclude that achieving the desired results requires alignment of multiple factors:

1. IT infrastructure
2. availability of data
3. suitable analytical models
4. compliance of frontline recruiters in executing the new practices.

For instance, the organization must have a reliable IT infrastructure to enable mobile access for recruiters and applicants. Similarly, a reliable IT infrastructure is needed for AI to learn from interactive input from the system users or for recruiters to get information and instructions based on AI to provide a personalized experience to applicants.

The organization also needs longitudinal data on individuals who have interacted with the system at each touch point, ranging from potential applicant status to work performance on the job, to train AI to estimate probabilities of success at these touch points using analytical models. This means that the organization must merge applicant data with employee data using PII. Without the longitudinally linked database, AI cannot use analytical models to estimate the potential suitability of applicants because it cannot predict how a potential applicant will perform if he or she accepts the job offer. For AI to be effective, it needs to learn from data input and the experiences of both applicants and recruiters.

A key factor connecting data-enabled technology with desired results is frontline marketers' and recruiters' use of data-enabled practices and compliance with specified procedures. Without their compliance with the requirements of the system, the return on capital investment in the development of technical capabilities will be incomplete. Therefore, Henke, Libarikian, and Wiseman, 2016, frame data-enabled business practices as a cultural change that must be led by top leaders of the organization.

CHAPTER FOUR

Key Capabilities Desired to Better Use Data-Enabled Outreach and Recruiting in the U.S. Department of Defense

Much like the commonalities in the services' reported marketing and recruiting activities, the discussions during both SME group meetings revealed common challenges in their endeavors to meet recruiting goals. The services commented on resource shortages—whether in manpower, dollars, or both—and, as a result, indicated that they were pursuing ways to gain efficiencies in their marketing and recruiting operations. Chapter Two provided examples of emerging practices that the services reported using to gain such efficiencies by focusing marketing efforts on the right touch points and messages and focusing recruiters on youth with both greater propensity to join and the desired characteristics.

Technology and new ways to reach the target audience are continually evolving. For example, as discussed in Chapter Three, in non-DoD marketing and recruiting settings, in addition to the types of information that DoD and the services collect, organizations draw extensive information from web behavior, other online behavior, and mobile and direct marketing interactions. Multiple first- and third-party sources are used to generate insights about demographics, psychographics, lifestyle, and media consumption characteristics for prospects. The SMEs in our workshops noted that attracting and recruiting candidates for the all-volunteer force could benefit from the ability to make broader use of data-enabled marketing and recruiting. This includes niche targeting and customized one-on-one messaging as practiced in the private sector, which rely on using PII and third-party data to microtarget potential recruits.

Niche Targeting and Customized One-on-One Messaging

The services and DoD indicated that they want to be able to take better advantage of third-party data and to integrate those data with their first-party data to enrich their marketing and recruiting operations. They indicated that this would enable them to develop deeper, more-granular target audience profiles. Using these more-detailed profiles, recruiters could better prioritize and target prospective recruits. Selection of media, touch points, and personalized messaging could then be refined for outreach and recruiting activities to reach these potential recruits and to guide interactions with them throughout the recruiting process. Recruiters could also initiate specific career field and job recruitment with highly targeted messaging and media touch points.

Better Targeting Prospects and Influencers Through Use of Personally Identifiable Information and Third-Party Data

The SMEs noted that better leveraging of PII and third-party data to microtarget potential recruits centers around being able to take advantage of what many commercial marketers do routinely. As we summarized in Chapter Three, a lot of information is collected by third-party data brokers. They build millions of individual profiles and append large amounts of data. This information includes biographical details, charitable giving, hobbies, purchases, personal finance, health, search engine history, and cookies, among others. These data can be segmented on many levels, including by locality, household, and individual. Third parties cross-reference data gathered from web measurement and customization technologies (WMCT) against PII, including data obtained from websites (via analytic cookies and media tags). Unlike DoD agencies, third parties are not hampered by explicit user consent or opt-in requirements.

An example provided by the SMEs of using big data, including third-party data, to develop deeper, more-granular target audience profiles to prioritize and target prospective recruits, and to help select media and touch points to reach these prospects, involves providing email addresses to Facebook for one-to-one message targeting to personalize contacts. As part of this effort, the services could initiate more-targeted career field and job-specific recruitment with highly targeted messaging and media touch points.

More generally, the services indicated that, to enable more-personalized contacts, another useful cross-referencing step would be to cross-reference data gathered from WMCT against PII to determine online activity at the individual level. This would help the services to use third-party data and PII to personalize communications across multiple touch points in the prospect and lead phases of the recruiting process. For example, the Air Force talked about the lack of a robust CRM capability, which limits its ability to capture an individual's history of interactions with the Air Force across multiple touch points. Such a capability would enable deeper audience insights, more-personalized and timely communication streams, and improved user experience—for prospects, leads, recruits, and recruiters. This improved communication would enable an in-depth analysis of the entire customer journey from initial contact to contract signing. Such prospect relationship management would support appropriate messaging, touch points, and the rhythm of the recruiting process and could further improve recruiting efforts.

The SMEs also noted that because third parties own their data and may not wish to directly share their databases with the government, DoD components would ideally be allowed to more broadly cross-reference PII and tracking data across internet sites and data sources themselves. For example, the SMEs indicated that tracking user-level activity on the internet beyond one's DoD internet domain and then targeting individual communications to .com or .edu site visitors based on the pages and content of interest to them would facilitate targeted delivery of messages to this important broader audience. The SMEs further indicated that it also would be beneficial to share data with other federal agencies, the DoD components, and other government organizations. Members of the DoD Privacy Program/PII workshop indicated that it would be helpful if the military recruiting system could target influencers using PII from associated influencers, such as counselors, teachers, coaches, and school principals.

Another ability to make broader use of PII in data-enabled marketing and recruiting that the services would like involves text messaging. Although text messaging has become increasingly popular as a means of real-time, individualized communication and information exchange, the services reported that the degree to which they can use it as desired for military recruiting is unclear, even when the prospective recruit provides the mobile number. This is because it involves using PII to provide information that the prospect might not have requested or might not have opted in to having sent via text messaging. The Navy reported that it faced a lawsuit after Navy options were sent via text to such a prospect. Although no action was taken against the Navy, these types of situations concern the services and, therefore, limit their text usage.

The Army discussed the need to bridge the gap between broad marketing efforts at the national level, to build awareness and communicate the Army message, and developing outreach and recruiting practices at the local level. A related gap concerns the collection of data for generalizability at the national level versus collecting data providing insights for key subgroups of interest, such as 17- and 18-year-olds, as well as the level of aggregation of the available data. The data currently available to guide marketing for the 17- and 18-year-old cohort, which is of particular interest to recruiters, are less robust than desired, according to the SMEs. Moreover, they indicated that data are often limited to ZIP codes. Many of the DoD survey and national measures available do not even measure outcomes at the ZIP code level. This makes it difficult to gain a micro-level picture of propensity to join and potential recruits' interests and concerns—something needed geographically by the reserve components, given that they recruit for units within a 50- to 100-mile radius of a prospective recruit's location, and, more generally, for active component recruiting. Another example is the desire to get ROTC information to students when they are making college decisions. This desire also is not in sync with the national campaign age group composition and data collection because students are making college decisions throughout their high school years. There needs to be a mechanism to reach those students and their influencers with the right information at the right times and places while remaining within prescribed recruiting outreach policies.

Experimental Assessment of the Potential Value of New Variables and Technology

A major desired capability voiced during the DoD Privacy Program/PII workshop was the ability to temporarily add new variables or technology to a data collection effort so that their value could be assessed before going through the full effort required to change the related System of Records Notice (SORN) required by DoD policies (see Chapter Five). The participants indicated that changing and obtaining approval for the modified SORN can be a very lengthy and time-consuming process, so lengthy that it could prevent the new variables or technology being tested from informing time-sensitive decisions, and so time consuming that changing the SORN prior to assessing the usefulness of the new variables or technology could waste valuable time and resources.

Cloud-Based Computing and Other Information Technology Improvements

The services expressed their desire for greater use of cloud technology to store information. They indicated that limitations in this area make it difficult to leverage industry methods and best practices and to keep pace with the latest technology. The Army discussed limits on its current ability to share data and the need for greater cloud-based storage to eliminate such barriers, including the need for a system through which the active and reserve components could share data. A broad, cloud-based system would allow the Regular Army, Army Reserve, and ARNG mobile access to data and analysis tools. The Army's new accessions data system, AIE, will provide a cloud-based solution for accessions data that is readily accessible.

Recruiters indicated their desire for more-modern systems that could better support them and improve the efficiency of their work, such as systems and tools that support increased interconnectivity, mobility, and updated means of technology-based communication with youth. This includes updated technology and related policies to reflect the role of social media and other technology-based communication used by youth. The Army's Enterprise Total Asset Visibility (ETAV) recruiting tool is a current step in that direction. It assists recruiters and allows them to be more mobile by enabling them to enter and receive information on potential recruits in real time using cloud-based computing technology. The goal is to move away from paper and to use digital data. USAREC reports that it is faster to update and use, more efficient, easier to manipulate, and easier to control and secure. ETAV is available to active and reserve recruiters. It is a bridging strategy until the Army gets the AIE product fully deployed.

Another example is a CRM platform. With a CRM platform, the data could be accessed directly from a variety of hubs while being drawn from a central source and would put a wide variety of data at the recruiter's fingertips. As discussed above, it would also allow recruiters to initiate more job-specific recruitment with highly targeted messaging, media, and touch points, further optimizing recruiter efforts.

CHAPTER FIVE

Challenges Associated with Better Use of Data-Enabled Outreach and Recruiting in the U.S. Department of Defense

Much like the commonalities in the services' reported marketing and recruiting activities, the discussions during the advisory group and DoD Privacy Program/PII meetings and in the recruiter focus groups revealed common challenges in their endeavors to meet recruiting goals. The previous chapter provided examples of capabilities that the services and DoD would like to use to help gain outreach and recruiting efficiencies by focusing marketing efforts on the right touch points and messages and focusing recruiters on youth with both greater propensity to join and the desired characteristics. However, information concerning DoD and service use of data-enabled and internet-based efforts provided by our study SMEs points to slower progress than desired and to several contributing factors for that slower progress. They include issues associated with using PII and emerging technologies, related data limitations, IT infrastructure deficiencies, historical trends rather than data analytics driving current practices, and a lack of feedback on the success of outreach and recruiting operations. These factors reflect problems in the general areas referenced in Chapter Three as underlying successful achievement of data-enabled outreach and recruiting.

We summarize main points from the SME and recruiter discussions about inhibiting factors below. We discuss specific challenges posed to data-enabled outreach and recruiting by the Privacy Act's

SORN process (5 USC 552a[4]); 10 USC 503,[1] which limits DoD's ability to collect information beyond the directory level;[2] and OMB M-10-22 and DoD Instruction 8550.01 Section f (1)(b), which provide guidance and limits on use of WMCT.

DoD Privacy Program

DoD is held to data, technology, and policy regulations that limit its capabilities in using data-enabled outreach and recruiting, putting it at a disadvantage in comparison with civilian marketers in the corporate sector and impeding potential efficiencies. JAMRS, for example, does not use analytics to combine information from different data sources. The services all have procedures in place to protect PII in accordance with service and government policies. These procedures generally focus on restricted access and controls for compliance. The Navy, for example, has procedures associated with prospecting and processing applicant information that address PII and the potential aggregation of multiple data. Regardless of the approach that DoD and the services use in their recruiting efforts, protecting PII and following the SORN process in accordance with the Privacy Act remain a consistent requirement.

DoD could make more use of data-enabled outreach and recruiting practices if permitted to do so. Even though the services are executing some practices that are consistent with these approaches, many of

---

1 Organizations in the different sectors must comply with specific legal restrictions and regulations in their usage of big data. For instance, financial institutions must comply with the Gramm-Leach-Bliley Act, 1999. Similarly, in the health care sector, organizations must comply with the Health Insurance Portability and Accountability Act. In addition, there are state and local privacy and data security laws, such as the California Online Privacy Protection Act, and regulations, such as the Massachusetts Data Security regulations.

2 *Directory information* follows the definition under Section 444 of the General Education Provisions Act, as amended through Public Law 114-95. It includes "name, address, telephone listing, date and place of birth, major field of study, participation in officially recognized activities and sports, weight and height of members of athletic teams, dates of attendance, degrees and awards received, and the most recent previous educational agency or institution attended by the student."

the barriers to the capabilities they desire to more fully use big data and PII (discussed in Chapter Four) reflect restrictions under OMB M-10-22 and DoD Instruction 8550.01 that restrict the department from

- tracking users' individual-level activity on the internet outside of one's DoD domain
- sharing data with other federal agencies, DoD components, or other organizations without explicit consent from individuals
- cross-referencing data gathered from WMCT against PII to determine individual-level online activity.

Over the next five to ten years, how to best harness the power of big data to microtarget the youth population is likely to be a significant outreach and recruiting issue. Indeed, as noted, capability requirements for the Army's new AIE include leads scoring and prioritization software built into the system and AI to help in that process, and USAREC is exploring pilot projects with industry that use AI for data analysis and engagement strategies. The desired use of big data will require relief from directory information–level limitations on data collection under 10 USC 503 and on WMCT and third-party data use under OMB M-10-22 and DoD Instruction 8550.01. It also will necessitate multiple groups (legal, privacy, civil liberties, IT, and others) working together to reexamine authority structure; identify what data elements are useful and necessary for military outreach and recruiting, including ROI; ensure flexible and efficient SORN processes; update IT infrastructure requirements and safeguards if and as needed; and consider when third-party data should be used. Internal issues also need to be addressed regarding those who can access and use the data: who has the need to know, the access rules, local use, and global use.

In Chapter Three, we observed that big data that captures important aspects of our daily life is an essential element of data-enabled recruiting practices, as is the ability to improve the practices' effectiveness over time by learning from the experience and insights of the users of the system. Organizations cannot assemble big data without the capability to merge databases by matching information about individuals from a variety of data sources, including third-party data.

Hence, PII is an enabling factor that animates the creation of big data. And data-enabled outreach and recruiting practices cannot evolve on an ongoing basis without the flexibility to adjust the information and analytic tools they rely on in response to user input concerning their utility and the opportunity to leverage additional information and evolving technologies.

Given the challenges outlined above, RAND NDRI researchers worked closely with the sponsor and services to identify and convene a meeting of key stakeholders, including legal, privacy, and policy experts and relevant DoD and service representatives. On January 11, 2018, RAND hosted a workshop with these stakeholders. The purpose of the attendees' presentations and related discussions was to look specifically at the DoD Privacy Program; implementation of this program; data collected by the services and DoD, with particular focus on PII; how digital information that includes PII is currently used for military recruiting purposes; additional data collection, data mining and analysis, and technological capabilities that the DoD Privacy Program/PII SMEs believed would better allow them to use big data and PII; constraints to such leveraging of PII and big data in military recruiting; and key actions that could be taken or requested by DoD to facilitate such use of new information and technology in data-enabled outreach and recruiting practices. Table 5.1 lists the organizations that participated in the DoD Privacy Program/PII workshop.

We discussed earlier the data collected by the services and DoD; how digital information that includes PII is currently used for military recruiting purposes; and additional data collection, data mining and analysis, and technological capabilities desired to better use big data and PII in military outreach and recruiting practices. Key actions to facilitate such use of data-enabled marketing and recruiting practices are discussed in Chapter Six. In this chapter, we look specifically at issues discussed by the SMEs in the DoD Privacy Program/PII workshop, in the advisory group meeting, and in the recruiter focus groups that concern the DoD Privacy Program; implementation of this program; and constraints to leveraging big data and PII in military outreach and recruiting. The issues include the restrictions under the Privacy Act, 10 USC 503, OMB M-10-22, and DoD Instruction 8550.01.

Table 5.1
Organizations Participating in DoD Privacy Program/ PII Workshop

Organizations
Defense Privacy, Civil Liberties, and Transparency Division
Defense Human Resources Activity
OSD/Office of the General Counsel
OSD/Accession Policy
JAMRS
Mullen Lowe
Navy
Marine Corps
USAREC
AMRG
ARNG
Air Force[a]
IDA
RAND Corporation

[a] The Air Force participated subsequently by providing briefing slides on its experiences and issues.

Privacy Act

The Privacy Act of 1974 (5 USC 552a[4]) establishes a Code of Fair Information Practice that governs the collection, maintenance, use, and dissemination of PII that is maintained in *systems of records* by federal agencies, including DoD (U.S. Department of Justice, 2015). The Defense Privacy, Civil Liberties, and Transparency Division is responsible for ensuring that DoD complies with the Privacy Act. Table 5.2 lists official sources of privacy authorities and guidance.

The Privacy Act of 1974 states that agencies can only maintain information about an individual that is "relevant and necessary" to accomplish the agency's purpose or that is required by statute or

Table 5.2
Privacy Authorities and Guidance

Sources
The Privacy Act of 1974, 5 USC 552a
OMB Circular A-108 (December 2016b)
OMB Circular A-130 (July 28, 2016a)
DoD Directive 5400.11 (October 29, 2014)
DoD Regulation 5400.11-R (May 14, 2007)
OMB, "Privacy Act Implementation-Guidelines and Responsibilities," 40 FR 29849-28978 (July 9, 1975)
U.S. Department of Justice, "Overview of the Privacy Act of 1974"

executive order (5 USC 552 [e][1]). The Privacy Act also recommends that information that may result in an adverse determination about a right, benefit, or privilege be collected directly from an individual (5 USC 552 [e][2]). Thus, the Privacy Act is an overarching statute for privacy practice. For DoD, recruiting is essential to the mission, so that validates the need to collect PII.

Other publications provide implementation guidance for the Privacy Act. OMB circulars provide implementation guidance for all federal agencies (Circular A-108 [OMB, 2016b] and Circular A-130 [OMB, 2016a]). Within DoD, a directive (DoD Directive 5400.11, 2014) and regulation (DoD Regulation 5400.11-R, 2007) provide departmental implementation guidance. There is additional guidance available in other sources, but these date back to the mid-1970s, before the advent of modern computers, and are likely out of date for practical purposes.

Definitions

OMB defines *PII* as "information that can be used to distinguish or trace an individual's identity, either alone or when combined with other information that is linked or linkable to a specific individual" (OMB, 2016a). Unique file data, such as Social Security numbers, names, addresses, and telephone numbers are all PII. A single piece of information such as those noted might be an identifier. Other information not considered PII in itself, such as demographic information, also can become PII when combined with additional information and must then be managed as such, if the combined information can be used to identify an individual. Table 5.3 provides key privacy-related terms and their definitions.

The Privacy Act of 1974 defines *records* as "any item, collection, or grouping of information about an individual that is maintained by an agency" (5 USC 552a[4]). This includes paper or electronic records, such as employment records, educational records, financial records, medical history, or criminal history. A system of records is any group of records from which information is retrieved by the name of an individual or other PII assigned to an individual (5 USC 552a[4]).

Table 5.3
Key Definitions

Term	Definition
Individual	A citizen of the United States or an alien lawfully admitted for permanent residence (5 USC 552a[2])
PII	Information that can be used to distinguish or trace an individual's identity, either alone or when combined with other information that is linked or linkable to a specific individual (OMB, 2016a)
Record	Any item, collection, or grouping of information about an individual that is maintained by an agency (5 USC 552a[4])
System of records	A group of any records under the control of any agency from which information is retrieved by the name of the individual or by some identifying number, symbol, or other identifying particular assigned to the individual (5 USC 552a[4])
SORN	The notice(s) published by an agency in the Federal Register upon the establishment and/or modification of a system of records describing the existence and character of the system. A SORN identifies the system of records, the purpose(s) of the system, the authority for maintenance of the records, the categories of records maintained in the system, the categories of individuals about whom records are maintained, the routine uses to which the records are subject, and additional details about the system (OMB, 2016b).

The Privacy Act of 1974 requires that a federal agency publish a SORN in the Federal Register upon the establishment and/or modification of a system of records. Essentially, a SORN is intended to provide transparency to a system of records so that the public is aware of what data are being collected, why, and how those data are intended to be used. The Defense Privacy, Civil Liberties, and Transparency Division manages this process in DoD. Table 5.4 shows the items that must be included in a SORN.

Table 5.4
Elements of a System of Records Notice

Elements
System identifier
System name
Security classification
Categories of individuals covered by the system
Categories of records in the system
Authority for maintenance of the system
Purpose(s)
Routine uses of records maintained in the system, including categories of users and the purposes of such uses
Disclosure to consumer reporting agencies
Policies and practices for storing, retrieving, accessing, retaining, and disposing of records in the system
Safeguards
System manager and address
Notification procedure
Record access procedures
Contesting record procedures
Record source categories
Exemptions claimed for the system

Implementation of DoD Privacy Program

When data are collected, the Privacy Act requires the collecting organization to provide notice to the individual at the point of collection regarding the authority for the solicitation, the principal purpose, the effect of not providing the information, and authorizing information—the key points in the SORN. The Privacy Act also protects an individual's First Amendment rights. In addition, the Privacy Act requires agencies to establish appropriate safeguards to govern information storage, protection, retrieval, and disposal and to provide the public with information on how these safeguards will be maintained. Intentions to share information outside an agency must also be recorded in the SORN. DoD, for example, has a set of "routine uses" for which data can be shared outside DoD. All of these requirements are documented in the SORN to provide transparency to the public. Employees within federal agencies who collect and maintain the privacy of such data need to be trained on these requirements.

When an agency wants to collect new data, the SORN must be updated for each substantive change. Substantive changes include the authority to collect data, the purpose of the data, and a change in technology. Thus, system managers must consult with their privacy officials as to when system changes call for a revision to the SORN, and they must review potential changes to the SORN on a continual basis—a necessity driven by frequent technology changes, which can affect data collection, storage, retrieval, and safeguards.

Data Limitations

As discussed in Chapter Two, the services collect and retain a variety of recruiting-related data, much of it PII. This includes applicant information; recruiter-prospect interaction information, such as interview notes and attempted contacts; and information necessary to qualify an applicant for service accession programs. For example, the Marine Corps indicated that its recruiting process results in collection of 960 attributes for officers and 600 for potential enlistees—of which 540 are common to both. Not all of the information collected is PII, but once put into the recruiting information systems, the data are subject to a rigorous system of controls that protect the PII. In general, the services store the data in encrypted and limited-access processing systems. The Navy said that it is aiming in the future to reduce the number of systems that it uses to collect and process data.

JAMRS, which is located in the Office of People Analytics, plays a substantial role in harnessing big data capabilities in managing DoD talent, one component of which is to provide direct analytic support to OSD and the military services' recruiting efforts. A major effort reported to be underway was to scope the feasibility of creating a recruiting database for microtargeting. JAMRS currently collects a wide variety of individual and aggregate data from different sources, including a Joint Leads program and commercial sources, to provide the assembled data to all the services. JAMRS data sources include the High School Master File of juniors and seniors, previous DMDC collections, commercial list vendors, the ASVAB, the Selective Service System, and other commercial sources, such as college files. JAMRS' Joint Leads program contains information about individuals who indicate that they want more information about military service. The PII data collected by JAMRS includes directory information, full name, gender, and date of birth. Depending on source and availability, other PII information might include telephone number, school name, graduation date, grade point average, educational level, email address, military interest, college intent, ethnicity, ASVAB test date, registration method, and additional details.

Compared with organizations outside DoD, under the DoD Privacy Program and related guidance governing use of PII and WMCT, there are restrictions on what data can be collected and how such data can be collected and used by DoD. For example, JAMRS' authority to collect data comes from USC Title 10, but, as a DoD agency, it is restricted in the data it can collect. And details on what information JAMRS collects, why, and how it will be used must be provided in its required SORN. Access to these data is highly restricted and, under the Privacy Act, is limited to agencies requiring it in the performance of their official duties.

As discussed previously, the services rely on a mix of primary data collection and third-party data. But, under 10 USC 503, like JAMRS, they cannot collect information beyond the directory level. Constraints on the use of third-party data can limit its utility. For example, DoD policies governing PII limit access to information from third-party providers (see related discussion above). The restrictions on third-party data limit the depth of knowledge that the services can collect about where and how to market, including the richness of segmentation profiles. As noted in Chapter Four, without such information, the data available to guide marketing, including for the 17- and 18-year-old cohort, which is of particular interest to recruiters, are less robust than desired. Data are often limited to ZIP codes or even higher levels of aggregation. This makes it difficult to gain a micro-level picture of propensity to join and potential recruits' interests and concerns.

Constraints on the use of WMCT and third-party data under OMB M-10-22 and DoD Instruction 8550.01 also were reported to be problematic, limiting the depth of knowledge that the services can collect about which prospects and leads are the most promising and how to tailor their interactions with these potential recruits. As the Army discussed, this information could help recruiters manage the sheer volume of leads if used to identify those who are qualified and enable recruiters to prioritize leads that are most promising.

Figure 5.1 shows potential commercial data sources that could be available to DoD and the services if restrictions on use of third-party data were lessened.

Information Technology Infrastructure Deficiencies

In some cases, data limitations are a result of how the services internally organize their data collection and access. The Marine Corps and Navy explained how information that would be useful for understanding a recruit's experience from initial contact to contract is not fully accessible because of data entry and security issues. For example, data accessibility can be limited by stovepiping of their data systems (i.e., infrastructure design that limits information flow). We discuss this in

Figure 5.1
Potential Data Sources from the Private Sector

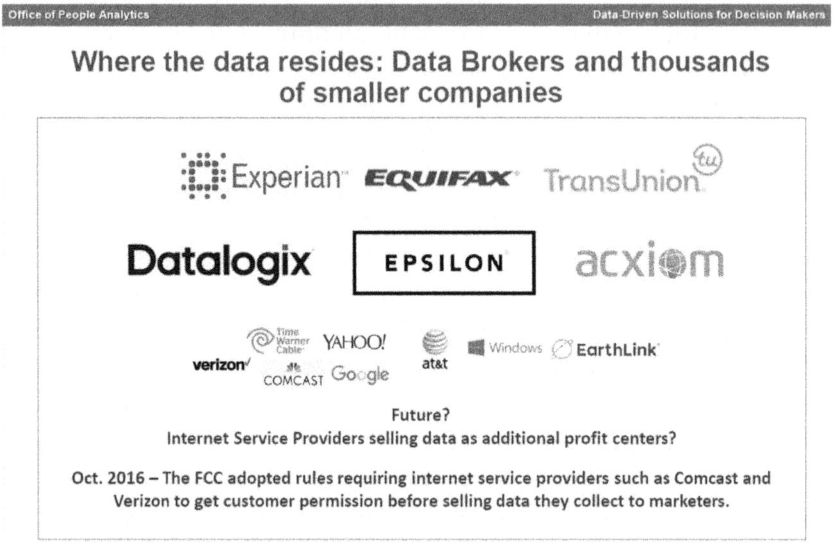

SOURCE: Mullen Lowe and Office of People Analytics.
NOTE: FCC = Federal Communications Commission.

more detail below. Ensuring input enforcement at the user level was reported to be another issue.

One of the infrastructure issues—which is connected to some degree with certain data limitations—is that many of the service data sets are disconnected from each other. This disconnection can result in access limitations, potentially preventing useful information from being used in planning and forecasting or in answering questions about why potential recruits dropped out of the process. It also can mean that the same data must be entered into multiple systems. The Navy discussed the challenges it faces even if both systems are certified to store and process the same data. As an example, it explained that its prospecting system does not talk to its processing system, which requires reentry of data and makes it impossible to determine the effect of prospecting efforts using these systems. Specifically, data collected by the National Advertising Lead Tracking System (NALTS) are not combined with recruiter sources of information. Thus, if a potential recruit provides a lot of information in NALTS and some time later walks into a recruiting station, the prospect is not treated as a lead, and his or her information is not accessible to the recruiter. This creates an inefficient process in which the recruiter is forced to re-collect and reenter the information. Another example reported by the Navy involves combination of information from Google, the Census, and the national college database to examine aggregate trends; there are restrictions on the amount of data that can be drawn down and shared. The Navy said that if such barriers were removed, it would be possible to improve analytical integration across logistics, finance, marketing, and recruiting operations; would increase the analytical support that could be provided to decisionmakers across the enterprise; and would support efficient use of recruiters' time. Similar situations were conveyed by the other services.

A related issue raised by the SMEs in the DoD Privacy Program/PII workshop involves the use of cloud technology to store information. Security-related concerns in this area make it difficult to leverage industry methods and best practices and to keep pace with the latest technology. The Army discussed limits on its current ability to share data and the need for greater cloud-based storage to eliminate such barriers, including the need for a system through which the active and reserve components could share data and that would provide mobile access to data and analysis tools. The decentralized nature of ARNG recruiting leads to significant challenges in maintaining data continuity from the states, territories, and the District of Columbia. Addressing such challenges would facilitate improved use of resources and open the door for more strategic analysis and greater use of predictive tools.

An area of key results from the recruiter focus groups concerned IT infrastructure issues at the local level. Participants in all focus groups across all service components raised issues related to IT infrastructure and how it limited recruiting activities. These systems were reported to restrict recruiters' mobility, flexibility, and ability to engage more frequently with potential recruits in the community.

Focus group participants expressed frustration when describing outdated IT systems and how they make recruiters' jobs much more difficult. One participant commented,

> [Our system] is slow—it crashes all the time. Additionally, it causes huge amounts of frustration, and crushing blows to recruiter morale when we have to work with applicants, and [the system], if it keeps crashing and it's slow, it makes them question our integrity when we have this 1995 system to process them to join the military. Things that should take 20 minutes will take an hour because of the system and the software—the servers that run the program are prehistoric.

Because of slow and outdated systems and lack of interconnectivity across systems, recruiters noted having to rely on paper copies and spend a great deal of time on service-mandated paperwork and entering information from hard copies into these systems and emphasized that this is a highly inefficient use of their time, the opposite of a recruiting force multiplier. For example, a few focus groups noted that mandated security clearance paperwork is particularly time consuming and frustrating for recruiters, who have to enter this information from hard-copy documents by hand into the computer system. One participant commented,

> I have to print out the security clearance by hand, fill it out [with the applicant], and type it in the system by hand, just to send them to MEPS. [The recruiters] have to do the clearance applications. So, if [the applicant] has multiple jobs or has been to [many] countries, it takes me three and a half hours to fill out the application just for the clearance.

Recruiters emphasized that they felt locked to their desks dealing with such paperwork because of the outdated IT systems.

Given the IT issues, recruiters had concerns related to the hard copies of documents that they must keep on hand that contain applicants' PII. Many participants felt that this information is not always secure in the current hard-copy system, whether it is in a cabinet back in the recruiting office or potentially left in a recruiter's car while he or she is out in the field during the day. Again, participants expressed that these potential PII issues were a result of outdated IT infrastructure that requires hard copies of documents containing PII. One participant described this issue as follows:

> We have to keep hard packets and hard copies that have Social Security numbers in my office, and they're locked in my cabinet, and you still have to have everything on your computer too. But, we have no cloud data storage, and if my computer crashes—that happened a few months ago and I lost everything. If I could back up [the information] and if it was encrypted or if we had a cloud platform—I'd rather have that than have the hard copies. There are people that have a key to my office, and they could steal Social Security numbers and all sorts of PII from the hard-copy documents. Even though we have a key to the office, the maintenance staff and security guards have keys too. Being a recruiter, you have access to all that personal information, and last thing I want is someone breaking in and taking that.

Some services noted a recruiting challenge related to the transparency of the vacancy system, which is, in part, an IT issue. Some focus group participants described frustration regarding this lack of transparency and stated that their ability to recruit individuals was impeded by not having the visibility of available jobs needed to match an applicant with a specific unit, job, or career field.

The services all agreed that infrastructure upgrades would go a long way toward increasing recruiter productivity. At the same time, they also acknowledged the difficulty involved in making the case for the resources that would need to be expended on infrastructure investments.

Analytical Tools

Another key area of focus group results concerns analytical tools used to support recruiting efforts. Recruiters reported a lack of advanced analytical tools. Rather, they reported that current tools, where available, tended to focus on tracking leads or applicants through the recruiting process. Many of these tools help to track student information or other leads, provide reminders to recruiters for contacting leads, and include background information on leads. Once an applicant has started the recruitment process, these tools may track where the applicant is in this process (e.g., forms that have been submitted, dates of MEPS visits) and track case file information. These tools were reported to serve primarily as organizational tools, and some also tracked the efficiency of recruiters (e.g., the length of time from the first contact to boot camp).

Participants generally did not mention tools that went much beyond organizational assistance. Tools described did not prioritize individuals or leads. As discussed earlier, recruiters indicated that they tend to make these prioritizations in an ad hoc manner at the local level. As also discussed regarding event prioritization in general, recruiters did not mention tools that would assist in prioritizing activities or events based on their ROI.

Recruiters reported that even when efforts have been made to provide a more mobile device, such as a tablet, intended to reduce paperwork and allow recruiters to be away from their desktop computers, the functionality was outdated and not helpful. One participant commented,

> The advantage of the tablet is supposed to be mobility. But we are still entering data. And when it comes to software updates, it has cut off our hands. The tablets become dinosaurs after a few years. All these extra features are out of touch with what we really need.

A participant from another focus group and a different service echoed this comment.

> It's a great idea with the tablets, but there is not a lot of follow through. Like, we go to events and the tablets won't work, so we still have paper cards, and that is pretty much what we use. We have had the tablet for close to three years now, and they tell us we are supposed to use it, but it is down so often and doesn't work, or the site can be down, so we would rather just use paper. We should get rid of the tablets—they are basically paperweights.

Participants discussed that if IT systems better supported these types of tools that were intended to increase their mobility and flexibility, they would actually be useful. But confidence in outdated local IT systems was low across the board. Similarly, when we asked focus group participants about using advanced analytical tools or big data to increase the effectiveness and efficiency of recruiting activities, participants reported that, while use of such tools and data could be helpful in principle, they did not believe that their local IT systems could support the use of advanced analytical tools or big data, and, therefore, they felt that near-term investments would be better spent upgrading and interconnecting current IT systems.

Historical Trends Driving Current Practice

We noted in Chapter Three that a potential barrier to successful use of data-enabled outreach and recruiting practices involves an organization's practices being constrained by historical policies and past behavior. During the advisory group presentations, the services indicated their tendency to focus recruiting efforts in areas where they have been successful in the past, such as regional segments of the market or particular educational establishments. While this approach is logical and has been relatively successful in meeting accession targets, the representatives from the services expressed concern that societal changes may make traditional approaches less successful in the future. These societal changes include shifts in the race/ethnicity distribution of the youth population, as visible in Census information, which numerous JAMRS surveys of the youth population and their influencers show is associated with differences in interest in joining the military, reasons for doing so, concerns, and support for joining. As noted by the services, Census data also indicate some shift in the population from more-rural areas to urban and suburban centers. The effects of this shift may be felt most by the reserve components because of their need to recruit within a close geographic area from reserve unit locations. But these location shifts could ultimately affect all the components because relocation from more- to less-isolated areas may present more employment alternatives for youth.

The Marine Corps talked about its tendency to rely on the same populations year after year and the need to expand its target audience beyond those populations. It reasoned that individuals who have not traditionally been interested in joining the military but perhaps are interested in public service might be persuaded to consider military service if the messaging were focused less on warfighting and more on humanitarian- and disaster-relief-oriented missions. The Marine Corps reported that, in 2012, it launched a marketing campaign with just such an aim. "Toward the Sound of Chaos" used social media, television commercials, and print ads to show the full spectrum of the Marine Corps' missions, including delivering humanitarian aid following wars, famine, or natural disasters—a campaign oriented toward individuals drawn to organizations like Habitat for Humanity. In recent years, Army marketing has also covered the breadth of its mission. This type of messaging could be adopted more widely by the services when the need to target new audiences with noncombat job interests becomes increasingly compelling.

Lack of Feedback

A key to successful data-enabled outreach and recruiting that we discussed in Chapter Three involves continual feedback on the elements of the organization's outreach and recruiting efforts concerning what is working well and what is not. Many of the services talked about how the lack of feedback on what is and is not working well in their outreach and recruiting practices constrains their ability to improve recruiting processes. The lack of feedback affects the system in a variety of ways. For example, many forecasting models are static models, and there is no mechanism by which insights from recruiters can be incorporated into those models and used to improve them. Addressing the data and infrastructure challenges just discussed could help to provide feedback, better enabling recruiters to develop more-granular target audience profiles, to identify more-desirable prospective recruits, and to use more-refined touch point selection to reach those audiences and prospects.

As discussed in Chapter Four (Army) and in this chapter (Navy), some of the services reported challenges in synchronizing efforts from the national to the local levels and stated that they lacked a feedback loop between them.

Feedback from potential and recent recruits is also important. Several of the services talked about recruit satisfaction surveys to provide insight into how their recruiters are doing, what is working well, and what is not. JAMRS, for example, carries out surveys with recent recruits to collect such information, including reasons for joining. Getting information from non-joiners is also important. The Marine Corps said that it has periodically conducted a non-joiner survey, but it is not updated on a regular basis. The Army also talked about its interest in understanding why it loses potential recruits after they express initial interest to capture more of them, including why recruits do not finish applications after they start the process. Conducting new surveys creates a data collection and recording burden, which becomes an additional duty and has related costs. Such concerns can be addressed by leveraging current internet technology that allows such information to be collected online in a way that is not labor- or cost-intensive, as well as by creating a sampling strategy in which every recruiter does not have to get survey responses from every potential recruit. Periodic selection could provide the desired information while relieving much of the burden.

Another issue regarding lack of feedback is incompleteness of data entry. Some recruiters in our focus groups indicated that they would not enter low-priority leads resulting from a school visit or other outreach activity into any kind of formal tracking system provided by the service. If they felt that individuals were not good leads and did not want to spend time following up with them, they did not want to be penalized for not doing so in a timely manner by any kind of service tracking system. One participant commented,

> The reason why we don't put some leads in [the system] is because, say, we have 70 leads, and we have to contact them all within five days. I still keep track of them by paper, but I don't want 70 leads

> on the books because then I'll be responsible for them. It's an undue burden.

Understanding and enhancing the value of outreach approaches requires information on both their positive and negative outcomes when the resources expended are driven by both types of outcomes.

CHAPTER SIX

Implications for Facilitating Greater Use of Data-Enabled Outreach and Recruitment Practices in the U.S. Department of Defense

Desired Capabilities to Better Use Data-Enabled Outreach and Recruiting

As discussed in earlier chapters, during the advisory group meeting of representatives from the services' recruiting operations divisions and marketing programs and the meeting of DoD Privacy Program/PII SMEs to discuss the DoD Privacy Program and related restrictions on data-enabled outreach and recruiting, the services and agencies indicated their desire for several key capabilities to enable them to increase use of data-enabled outreach and recruiting approaches. They include

- better targeting of prospects and influencers through use of PII and third-party data
- niche targeting and customized one-on-one messaging
- experimental assessment of the potential value of new variables and technology
- cloud-based computing and other IT improvements.

The SMEs indicated that the first capability would enable them to develop deeper, more-granular target audience profiles, and that, with these more detailed profiles, recruiters would be better able to prioritize prospective recruits and target them. They added that the second capability would help them to refine their selection of media, touch points, and personalized messaging in outreach and recruiting activities to reach these potential recruits and to guide interactions with them throughout the recruiting process. They also reported that these capabilities could enable them to initiate specific career field and job recruitment with highly targeted messaging and media touch points. The SMEs further indicated that to enable more-personalized contacts, another useful step would be to cross-reference data gathered from WMCT against PII to determine online activity at the individual level. This would help them to use third-party data and PII to personalize communications across multiple touch points in the prospect and lead phases of the recruiting process.

A major desired capability voiced during the DoD Privacy Program/PII workshop was the ability to temporarily add new variables or technology to a data collection effort in order to assess their value before undertaking the full effort required to change the related SORN required by DoD policies. Participants noted that, given the length of this change process, time-sensitive applications of the variables or technology could be missed, and, alternatively, that inability to test their value before undertaking a SORN revision could waste resources over the longer term.

The SMEs indicated that a broad, cloud-based system would provide the multiple components of a service with mobile access to data and analysis tools. Recruiters expressed their desire for more-modern systems and tools to better support them and improve the efficiency of their work, enabling increased interconnectivity, mobility, and updated means of technology-based communication with youth, including social media. A CRM platform would allow data to be accessed directly from a variety of hubs while being drawn from a central source. This could put a wide variety of data at the recruiters' fingertips. As discussed earlier, it would also allow recruiters to initiate more job-specific recruitment with highly targeted messaging, media, and touch points, further helping to optimize recruiter efforts.

Challenges Associated with Better Use of Data-Enabled Outreach and Recruiting in the U.S. Department of Defense

During the advisory group meeting of representatives from the services' recruiting operations divisions and marketing programs, the meeting of DoD Privacy Program/PII SMEs, and focus group discussions with recruiters, several challenges to increased use of data-enabled outreach and recruiting were raised. They include

- the Privacy Act
- guidance on implementation of the DoD Privacy Program
- data limitations
- IT infrastructure deficiencies
- analytical tools
- historical trends driving current practice
- lack of feedback.

Specific challenges posed to data-enabled outreach and recruiting by the Privacy Act's SORN process; 10 USC 503, which limits DoD's ability to collect information beyond the directory level; and OMB M-10-22 and DoD Instruction 8550.01 Section f (1) (b), which provide guidance and limits on use of WMCT, were noted and discussed. Restrictions under OMB M-10-22 and DoD Instruction 8550.01 restrict DoD from

- sharing data with other federal agencies, the DoD components, or other organizations without explicit consent from individuals
- tracking users' individual-level activity on the internet outside of one's DoD domain
- cross-referencing any data gathered from WMCT against PII to determine individual-level online activity.

As discussed earlier, the services and defense programs that support military recruiting, such as JAMRS, rely on a mix of primary data collection and third-party data, but, under 10 USC 503, they cannot collect information beyond the directory level. They reported that constraints on the use of third-party data can limit the data's utility. For example, DoD policies governing PII limit access to information from third-party providers, which restricts the depth of knowledge that the services and defense programs can collect about where and how to market. As noted in Chapter Four, data are often limited to ZIP codes or even higher levels of aggregation. This makes it difficult to gain a micro-level picture of propensity to join and potential recruits' interests and concerns.

Constraints on the use of WMCT and third-party data under OMB M-10-22 and DoD Instruction 8550.01 were also reported to be problematic, limiting the depth of knowledge that the services can collect about which prospects and leads are the most promising and use to tailor their interactions with these potential recruits. As the Army discussed, this information could help recruiters manage and prioritize the sheer volume of leads by identifying those who are qualified and are the most promising.

One of the infrastructure issues—which is connected with certain data limitations—is that many service data sets are disconnected from each other. This can result in access limitations, potentially preventing information from being used in planning and forecasting or in answering questions about why potential recruits dropped out of the process. It also can mean that the same data have to be entered into multiple systems. Participants in all recruiter focus groups across all service components raised issues related to IT infrastructure and how it limited recruiting activities. These systems were reported to restrict recruiters' mobility, flexibility, and ability to engage more frequently with potential recruits in the community. Recruiters also reported a lack of advanced analytical tools. They reported that current tools, where available, tended to focus on tracking leads or applicants through the recruiting process.

A related issue raised by the SMEs in the DoD Privacy Program/PII workshop involves the use of cloud technology to store information. Security-related concerns in this area make it difficult to leverage industry methods and best practices and to keep pace with the latest technology.

During the advisory group presentations, the services discussed their tendency to focus recruiting efforts in areas where they had been successful, whether it be regional segments of the market or particular educational sites. They expressed concern that changes in the youth population, such as race/ethnicity mix and geographical distribution, could make traditional approaches less successful in the future. The Marine Corps also discussed the need for broader content in messaging as the need to target new audiences with non-combat job interests becomes increasingly compelling.

Many of the services talked about how the lack of feedback on what is working well and what is not in their outreach and recruiting practices constrains their ability to improve recruiting processes. Some of the services reported challenges in synchronizing efforts from the national to the local levels and stated that they lacked a feedback loop between them.

Key Actions to Facilitate Use of Data-Enabled Outreach and Recruitment Practices in the U.S. Department of Defense

Continue to Share Information Across the Services, the U.S. Department of Defense, and Marketing Agencies About Their Data-Enabled Outreach and Recruiting Practices to Broaden Their Use

During the advisory group and DoD Privacy Program/PII meetings, the services indicated that they were pursuing data-enabled efficiencies in their marketing and recruiting operations by using data analytics to inform their outreach and recruiting activities. The specific uses of data and analytics discussed by the SMEs varied across services. Wider adoption of emerging data-enabled outreach and recruiting practices would reduce dependence on historical practices.

Some services reported using mapping applications that allow recruiters to visualize promising recruiting zones and location-specific trends. They reported that their use of social media is increasing. Most have developed a social media presence at the service level and at the recruiter level. Individual recruiters build virtual networks, gain a following, and follow others to create a sense of authenticity about military service. To save recruiters' time, the Army's LRC prequalifies leads and scores them on multiple dimensions, enabling recruiters to prioritize leads for follow-up. The Army's VRC supports local recruiting efforts and can be used to target individuals or groups to fill particular needs.

Improve the Interconnectivity of Information Technology Systems, Recruiting Databases, and Tools

Numerous participants in this research noted the utility of improving the interconnectivity of IT systems, recruiting databases, and tools. They reported that the lack of interconnectivity can limit the visibility of important data within and between echelons and functions, which, in turn, can cause duplication of effort, limit recruiters' time to engage in recruiting activities, and impede assessment and adoption of the best outreach and recruiting activities. Moreover, the DoD Privacy Program/PII experts reported that many of the people, influencers, and prospective recruits that recruiters talk to are in the .com and .edu worlds. They thought it important to enable recruiters to reach people in those communities securely enough and in an up-to-date communication format and platform; this involves both PII and IT issues. Thus, near-term investments in IT upgrades and interconnectivity and in tools for recruiting (some of which would require IT and interconnectivity upgrades) could have a substantial ROI. DoD should determine which of these investments are most critical and actionable with respect to the associated cost and technological issues.

Increase Feedback Within the Outreach and Recruiting Processes

Many of the services talked about how the lack of feedback on the success of outreach and recruiting operations constrains their ability to improve recruiting processes. The services desired such feedback to develop more-granular target audience profiles, identify more-desirable prospective recruits, use more-refined touch point selection to reach those audiences and prospects, synchronize efforts from the national to the local levels, incorporate insights from recruiters into forecasting, and use feedback from potential and recent recruits on what is working well and what is not. The types of data and infrastructure deficiencies discussed above play a role in the lack of feedback.

Introduce Greater Flexibility into the System of Records Notice Development Process

Adjusting the SORN development process so that it can be broader and more flexible could have considerable value in supporting data-enabled outreach and recruiting. The DoD Privacy Program/PII SMEs reported that the current SORN process is becoming very restrictive in today's environment and should be modified. They noted that there are times when additional variables or tools might have temporary or long-term value that is not fully known without assessment, adding that a process to temporarily test something's value before going through the full effort required to change the SORN would be useful. They noted that this could be accomplished through an umbrella agreement—e.g., adding a routine uses phrase to SORNs that covered additional data and methods for mining and market research. Generic language could be used to allow for collecting data for testing purposes or testing new tools—in essence, to support experimentation. Another approach discussed was whether a broad SORN could be written for all DoD components and services to cover routine data collection and uses. This would provide more flexibility and reduce the services' workload but would require DoD to consider what level of joint recruiting it desires. Developing such an approach could be time consuming; thus, initially assessing a joint SORN'S feasibility would be appropriate.

Target Impediments to Data Collection, Including Using Third-Party Data and Personally Identifiable Information in Marketing and Recruiting

Another important action discussed by the DoD Privacy Program/PII SMEs is to address existing laws and policies that hamper DoD's ability to collect data beyond the directory level and to take advantage of third-party data and analytics. To fully leverage greater flexibility in the SORN process, as described in the preceding section, existing law under 10 USC 503 would need to be modified to allow the collection of data beyond the directory level. Also, the SMEs indicated that restrictions under OMB M-10-22 and DoD Instruction 8550.01 that limit the use of WMCT and third-party data must be addressed. As noted, these current policy restrictions focus on three areas: (1) tracking individual users outside of one's domain, (2) sharing data that DoD collects or tracks or sharing behavioral data without consent, and (3) cross-referencing web users' behavior.

The SMEs indicated that a change in authorities is needed to allow DoD to more fully use external sources and third-party data and to share individual lead and prospective recruit data with those sources so that they can then share more-complete data and analyses with DoD. With better access to such data and analytics, especially concerning what individuals were doing prior to becoming prospective recruits, the services could better target and customize the information provided to potential recruits. To enable DoD recruiting programs and the services to take full advantage of big data and machine learning, Congress, OMB, and DoD would need to broaden the authority to use those techniques and technologies. One approach could be for DoD to request a change in the guiding statute that would allow it to use outreach and recruiting practices employed outside DoD, such as those used in private industry. An initial, more-limited step could be for DoD to request Congress to allow the services to conduct pilot tests to investigate viable uses of third-party analytics, which would allow them to build the business case for broader changes. In an era of heightened privacy concerns, attention should be given to balancing greater authority to collect data and use it in niche targeting and customized messaging with the need to protect the privacy of youth and their influencers and avoid actions that could raise concerns about unwanted monitoring.

Routinely Evaluate the Effectiveness, Efficiency, and Acceptance of Data-Enabled Outreach and Recruiting Practices in Military Recruiting

As we discussed earlier, the potential transformative power of data-enabled marketing and recruiting through big data and AI is no longer conceptual or theoretical. Organizations are applying these practices. However, our knowledge about the efficiency and effectiveness of these practices in generating a greater number of leads or converting more leads into recruits in the military context is limited relative to what is known about the effectiveness of these practices in other areas, such as the usage of big data analytics in political campaigns (Nickerson and Rogers, 2014). If these practices have positive effects on recruiting outcomes, improvements in IT infrastructure or analytical capabilities, if necessary, might be costly. Also, if the quantity of leads and recruits increases because of the new practices, the quality and characteristics of these additional leads and recruits would then need to be assessed.

To ensure their successful implementation, the services need to prepare those directly involved in outreach and recruiting efforts to effectively use new tools in their daily work. As is true for any new technical innovation and new way of doing routine business—even when the recipients, such as recruiters, have noted their desire for more-modern systems that could better support mobility and flexibility and improve the efficiency of their work—the introduction of data-enabled practices can face resistance because their introduction will inevitably involve solving technical challenges and require new ways to accomplish familiar business outcomes, some of which may be welcome, and others less so.

It is important to note that data-enabled military outreach and recruiting practices could generate a negative reaction from some members of the targeted population, who might view the microtargeting efforts as a violation of privacy. While individuals may tolerate a private company microtargeting to sell its products, some could have a negative reaction to the services microtargeting youth for the purpose of recruitment (Segall, 2018).

APPENDIX A

Protocol for Focus Groups with Military Recruiters

RAND personnel conducted ten focus groups across all four services, including representation from active-duty and reserve component recruiters, primarily in the broader Los Angeles and Washington, D.C., metropolitan areas. RAND focus group facilitators began each session by providing background information on the study and administering informed consent. Focus group facilitators used the protocol below for this qualitative data collection effort and asked follow-up questions for clarity and to obtain additional information where appropriate based on the discussion.

Provide Study Overview and Administer Consent

General Background Questions

1. What is your service?
2. How long have you been a recruiter?
3. Would you consider the areas you typically recruit from urban, rural, or suburban?

Recruitment Process and Tools

We'd like to learn about the big data techniques or tools you use to guide your recruitment efforts during each stage of the process, from outreach to the contract signing.

4. What data analytics or tools do you use to guide you when you are determining where you should go to recruit or which recruiting events you should attend?
5. How do you keep track of leads that you acquire during recruiting events? (E.g., are these all entered into an electronic system?)
6. When you have leads from recruiting events, what data analytics or tools do you use to help prioritize these leads?
7. What type of data do you collect on leads?
8. What data science techniques do you use to compute ROI from recruiting events? Do you have a system or tool in place that establishes a feedback loop on the value of events?
9. What type of data do you collect on recruiting events?

Tool Value and Gaps

10. Of the data techniques or tools you mentioned, which have you found the most useful or effective? Why?
11. Are there gaps or challenges you face in recruiting that the current recruitment tools do not address?
12. Are there any other tools or data techniques you've seen used in other services or in the private sector that you wish you had access to?
13. For the tools you use and those you've seen, are there any concerns about personally identifiable information (PII) that have arisen?

APPENDIX B

Additional Detail on the Recruiting Process

This appendix provides additional information for the overview of the active enlisted recruiting process using the Air Force example discussed in Chapter Two. As noted, on average, a recruiter makes 110 contacts with potential candidates to produce one viable BMT recruit. Initial contact is divided into five categories: referrals, advertising leads, high school program leads, direct mail responses, and walk-ins. The process is linear, but a person can exit or reenter the funnel at each stage depending on the issue. For example, a person may be disqualified during the interview stage based on a low Enlisted Screening Test (EST) score or other disqualifying information. The same person may subsequently return, achieve a qualifying score, and proceed to the next step. The same is true for other steps in the process.

Types of Contacts

Types of contacts are defined as follows:

1. Referrals are candidates that the recruiter receives, from any source, who have expressed an interest in the Air Force.
2. Advertising leads are candidates drawn to a recruiter because of messaging received from a national, regional, or local advertising campaign (e.g., television or internet commercials, a NASCAR race, zone canvassing).

3. High school program leads are candidate referrals received from high school juniors or seniors who have already signed a contract to join the Air Force.
4. Direct mail responses are candidates who contact a recruiter based on literature (pamphlet, leaflet) received via U.S. Postal Services from Headquarters, Air Force Recruiting Service (HQ AFRS).
5. Finally, walk-in candidates are broadly characterized as people who engage a recruiter on their own initiative, without the influence of any Air Force outreach method.

Contact to Basic Military Training Process

Step 1: Contacts who express interest in moving forward with the process are prescreened to determine whether they meet basic eligibility criteria. Attrition at this stage is either terminal (stopping future processing) or temporary (the contact can continue with the process following a prescribed waiting period based on the issue).

Step 2: Next, contacts complete a face-to-face interview with the recruiter. Further descriptive background information is obtained during the interview. Here, the recruiter assesses the contact's financial responsibility (credit check), maturity level, whether the contact has an open application with another military service, tattoos that exceed the authorized size limitation on the applied body part, and EST scores. The EST is an abbreviated version of the official ASVAB and is used by recruiters to assess an applicant's ability to pass the ASVAB. Although the EST is not the official entry exam, contacts with low EST scores may attrite at this stage if the recruiter is not confident that they will receive a passing score on the ASVAB. Candidates who do not pass the ASVAB add additional time to an already stressed recruiter schedule. Time is lost to transportation, counseling, and mandatory wait time for retest, ranging from 30 days to six months.

Step 3: Candidates who move forward to take the ASVAB must receive a minimum AFQT score in order to advance. AFQT scores are computed using the standard scores from four ASVAB subtests:

arithmetic reasoning, mathematics knowledge, paragraph comprehension, and word knowledge. AFQT scores are reported as percentiles between 1 and 99.

Step 4: Next, applicants are screened by physicians at a MEPS for a myriad of medical conditions. Physicians review the applicant's medical history and perform a current physical examination for issues and conditions incompatible with military service. Incompatible medical conditions or a history of injuries or certain conditions will result in permanent or temporary (pending additional information needed for resolution) disqualification.

Step 5: Applicants who sign enlistment contracts after having successfully completed and passed the prescreen, interview, ASVAB, and MEPS physical will enter the DEP. The DEP is the final step before a recruit ships to BMT. In the Air Force, recruits may remain in the DEP for up to two years before ship day. The maximum and average lengths vary by service. During this time, numerous life events can result in the recruit's disqualification from military service. Top attrition issues include failure to graduate, new legal offenses, emerging health issues, and pregnancy.

The Air Force Recruiting Service (AFRS) does not officially track or assign a value to the number of candidates lost at each step. Anecdotal evidence suggests that most candidates attrite based on data collected during the interview, followed by disqualifying medical conditions discovered during the MEPS visit.

Lead Generation and Related Data

Leads are divided into two categories—national and local. AFRS and the Air Force's advertising agency are responsible for national lead generation. This is done through various outreach platforms. Local lead generation is the responsibility of the squadron and the recruiter. For all viable leads, prescreen data are collected and loaded to AFRISS-TF, the recruitment management system. Prescreen data include basic identity and contact information that allows recruiters to screen leads across broad eligibility categories (e.g., age, education) for follow-up consistent with the Air Force Recruiting Procedural Guide.

National Lead Generation

- AirForce.com is an Air Force–sponsored website that provides information on the Air Force experience. Visitors learn about the Air Force mission, education, more than 130 careers, and the Air Force lifestyle and are provided instructions on how to contact a recruiter and join.
- Mobile tours and events are managed as national leads for specific regions and zones. Air shows, NASCAR races, and snocross competitions are the most popular events. At these events, the Air Force rents booth space at which recruiters can engage patrons. These events draw a national audience and are specifically targeted based on patron demographics that strongly correlate to skills needed within the Air Force. For example, NASCAR patrons are sought after for their patriotism and mechanical aptitude. Leads from these events are considered Priority 1 and must be contacted within five days.
- National advertising occurs across all media. Current commercials appeal to a viewer's call to military service, interest in adventure, and educational opportunities. The advertising agency focuses advertising efforts on television shows, movies, and internet content with a viewer base consistent with the accession target demographic, 18–24 years of age.
- HQ AFRS produces direct mail material to help recruiters generate Priority 1 leads. Direct mail targets specific recipients via the U.S. Postal Service with either a letter or pamphlet that includes a mail-back response card. Direct mailers are a targeted communication approach aimed to motivate the recipient to respond and receive additional information about the Air Force. Respondents to direct mailers are considered a Priority 1 lead.
- The Air Force is in the final development stages of new online gaming technology. The Air Force plans to expand technology that was originally developed for pilot simulators to recruit

prospecting. The objective is to identify users with Air Force potential as demonstrated by skills used in the online game. While users will not be identified by name, the game will collect user interaction information and IP addresses as data points. The Air Force can then further advertise, gauge propensity, and potentially offer scholarship opportunities. The specifics of this medium are not fully defined. Other games are currently available on AirForce.com. Players can engage in a variety of missions that require them to select specific Air Force careers and capabilities to successfully complete the assigned challenge.

- The distinguished educator tour invites high school counselors, school administrators, teachers, coaches, community college professors, and school program managers to visit HQ AFRS. During the tour, educators receive a general overview of Air Force benefits, careers, and opportunities. The tour includes leadership briefings and interactive experiences with leaders from HQ AFRS, BMT, technical training, and the special operations community. Educators have provided feedback indicating that the tour and interaction with commanders, recruiters, and AFRS staff facilitated meaningful, one-on-one conversations with their students. They commented that the tour helped them to better discern and counsel students whom they believe will be a good fit for the Air Force.
- Chatters are retired, award-winning recruiters who now serve as online advisers and respond to those who express interest through airforce.com and the official Air Force Recruiting Facebook page. Chatters provide a central point of contact to field questions in a timely manner and forward leads.

Local Lead Generation

- Recruiters utilize PSA television or radio spots to increase awareness of the Air Force. PSAs are produced by HQ AFRS for message standardization and are aired on local television and radio stations.
- Telephone prospecting is the oldest and least-favorite lead-generating method. Public schools that receive federal funding

are required by law to provide student phone rosters to recruiters if asked. Typically, lists include the general student roster for juniors and seniors and a more focused list of students who have taken the ASVAB. Recruiters cold-call numbers provided to solicit interest in Air Force service.

- A *perpetuated lead* is a new lead referred by a previous candidate. The recruiting business relies on perpetuation to survive within a given market. A candidate or recruit who is excited about his or her experience and opportunities and shares that information with people within his or her circle of influence is important to a successful market. Influencers will have the greatest impact on a candidate's decision to join the Air Force.
- COI events engage prospective applicants and/or influence parents, teachers, counselors, coaches and other people critical to a student's decisionmaking process. Candidate-focused COI events encourage current DEP members to bring a friend, family member, or person open to learning about Air Force opportunities. The end goal is DEP expansion through perpetuation.
- Recruiters are responsible for Air Force brand awareness within their assigned zone. Zone canvassing requires the recruiter to establish and maintain a positive community rapport, be a known Air Force presence, and promote Air Force values and opportunities that best fit the local demographic. Canvassing occurs throughout the zone, but popular places to reach the target demographic are schools, malls, community centers, fitness centers, the Chamber of Commerce, and widely attended recurring local festivals.

Post-Lead Data Collection

As previously mentioned, during the face-to-face interview, detailed background information is collected on contacts. Information received is manually loaded by the recruiter to the contact's profile in AFRISS-TF. Post-interview data, such as ASVAB score, scores for job-specific tests, MEPS results, job preference, and job qualifiers, complete an applicant's profile. All information related to the individual candidate or recruit, the recruiting process, leadership expectations, and the assigned mission (goal) is managed within AFRISS-TF.

The recruiter's progress and the status of achieving the aggregate AFRS goal are evaluated and monitored through various reports generated from AFRISS-TF. A commonly used analysis tool is the flow trend report. It is produced and monitored at least monthly for each recruiter at the unit level. The flow trend report provides detailed statistics on the number of contacts, appointments, the ASVAB test pass rate, the MEPS success rate, the applicant cancellation rate, the new enlisted contract rate, and the entered active-duty rate. The data are used to counsel recruiters on successful trends and highlight areas for improvement. Flow trend data are also reviewed by the group and the AFRS Operations Analysis Branch. Additional ad hoc reports are pulled from AFRISS-TF on an as-needed basis as production indicators. Reports that reflect the number of leads assigned to a recruiter, the number of personal interview records not tested, the number who test qualified but not processed, MEPS activity, the number qualified and waiting, the number out of the DEP, the number in the DEP, the number who have entered active duty, cancellations, waivers, and MEPS recoverable losses are frequently used by the Operations Analysis Branch to provide an in-depth perspective on what works well and any potential challenges.

References

5 USC 552a—*See* U.S. Code, Title 5, Section 552a.

10 USC 503—*See* U.S. Code, Title 10, Section 503.

Akoka, Jacky, Isabelle Comyn-Wattiau, and Nabil Laoufi, "Research on Big Data—A Systematic Mapping Study," *Computer Standards and Interfaces*, Vol. 54, 2017, pp. 105–115.

Artun, Omer, and Dominique Levin, *Predictive Marketing*, Hoboken, N.J.: John Wiley & Sons, 2015.

Berkelaar, Brenda L., "Different Ways New Information Technologies Influence Conventional Organizational Practices and Employment Relationships: The Case of Cybervetting for Personnel Selection," *Human Relations*, Vol. 70, No. 9, 2017, pp. 1115–1140.

Bersin, Josh, "HR Technology Disruptions for 2018," Deloitte Consulting, 2017.

Chamorro-Premuzic, Thomas, Dave Winsborough, Ryne A. Sherman, and Robert Hogan, "New Talent Signals: Shiny New Objects or a Brave New World?" *Industrial and Organizational Psychology*, Vol. 9, No. 3, 2016, pp. 621–640.

Chui, Michael, Jaes Manyika, Mehdi Miremadi, Nicolaus Henke, Rita Chung, Pieter Nel, and Sankalp Malhotra, *Notes from the AI Frontier: Applications and Value of Deep Learning*, discussion paper, New York: McKinsey Global Institute, 2018. As of July 11, 2019:
https://www.mckinsey.com/featured-insights/artificial-intelligence/notes-from-the-ai-frontier-applications-and-value-of-deep-learning#0

Chui, Michael, and Brian McCarthy, *An Executive's Guide to AI*, New York: McKinsey Global Institute, 2018. As of July 11, 2019:
https://www.mckinsey.com/~/media/McKinsey/Business%20Functions/McKinsey%20Analytics/Our%20Insights/An%20executives%20guide%20to%20AI/Executives-guide-to-AI

Davenport, Thomas H., *Big Data @ Work: Dispelling the Myths, Uncovering the Opportunities*, Boston, Mass.: Harvard Business Review Press, 2014.

Davenport, Thomas H., and Jeanne G. Harris, *Competing on Analytics: The New Science of Winning*, Boston, Mass.: Harvard Business Review Press, 2017.

General Education Provisions Act, as amended through Public Law 114-95, Section 444, December 10, 2015. As of August 16, 2019: https://legcounsel.house.gov/Comps/General%20Education%20Provisions%20Act.pdf

Gramm-Leach-Bliley Act, Public Law 106-102, November 12, 1999. As of July 11, 2019: https://www.govinfo.gov/content/pkg/PLAW-106publ102/pdf/PLAW-106publ102.pdf

Gunter, Wendy Arianne, Mohammad H. Rezazard Mehrizi, Marleen Huysman, and Frans Feldberg, "Debating Big Data: A Literature Review on Realizing Value from Big Data," *Journal of Strategic Information Systems*, Vol. 26, 2017, pp. 191–209.

Hall, Jeremy, "Remarks to the RAND Recruiting Practices Study Advisory Group Meeting," Arlington, Va., January 25, 2017.

Health Insurance Portability and Accountability Act, Public Law 104–191, August 21, 1996. As of August 16, 2019: https://www.govinfo.gov/app/details/PLAW-104publ191

Henke, Nicolaus, Ari Libarikian, and Bill Wiseman, "Straight Talk About Big Data," *McKinsey Quarterly*, October 2016. As of July 11, 2019: https://www.mckinsey.com/business-functions/digital-mckinsey/our-insights/straight-talk-about-big-data

Hutson, Matthew, "AI Researchers Allege That Machine Learning Is Alchemy," *Science*, May 3, 2018. As of July 11, 2019: https://www.sciencemag.org/news/2018/05/ai-researchers-allege-machine-learning-alchemy

Indeed.com, "Interview with Susan Harker, VP of Global Talent Acquisition at Amazon," YouTube, September 2015. As of July 15, 2019: https://www.youtube.com/watch?v=kl2xdxGIjqg

Indeed.com Blog, "Infographic: How AT&T Transformed the Job Application Process and Saved $1M," July 2016.

Inside Amazon Videos, "Amazon Student Programs: Talent Acquisition Development Program," YouTube, May 2017. As of July 15, 2019: https://www.youtube.com/watch?v=AODGw2bXsCg

JAMRS—*See* Joint Advertising Market Research & Studies.

Joint Advertising Market Research & Studies, *Barriers to Recruiter Access in High Schools*, white paper, Alexandria, Va., 2017.

Knight, Will, "The Dark Secret at the Heart of AI," *MIT Technology Review*, April 11, 2017. As of July 11, 2019:
https://www.technologyreview.com/s/604087/the-dark-secret-at-the-heart-of-ai/

Laney, Doug, "3D Data Management: Controlling Data Volume, Velocity, and Variety," *Application Delivery Strategies*, No. 949, Stamford, Conn.: META Group, February 6, 2001. As of July 11, 2019:
https://blogs.gartner.com/doug-laney/files/2012/01/ad949-3D-Data-Management-Controlling-Data-Volume-Velocity-and-Variety.pdf

L'Heureux, Alexandra, Katarina Grolinger, Hany F. Elyamany, and Miriam A. M. Capretz, "Machine Learning with Big Data: Challenges and Approaches," *IEEE Access*, Vol. 5, 2017, pp. 7776–7797.

Marjani, Mohsen, Fariza Nasaruddin, Abdullah Gani, Ahmad Karim, Ibrahim A. T. Hashem, Aisha Siddiqa, and Ibrar Yaqoob, "Big IoT Data Analytics: Architecture, Opportunities, and Open Research Challenges," *IEEE Access*, Vol. 5, 2017, pp. 5247–5261. As of July 11, 2019:
https://ieeexplore.ieee.org/stamp/stamp.jsp?tp=&arnumber=7888916

Maurer, Roy, "Tailor Recruiting Best Practices for Service-Sector Hiring," Alexandria, Va.: Society for Human Resource Management, November 2015.

Mayer, Elyse, "Be Better in Recruitment: Do as Amazon Does," *Smashfly Blog*, July 23, 2015. As of August 16, 2019:
http://blog.smashfly.com/2015/07/23/be-better-in-recruitment-do-as-amazon-does/

McAfee, Andrew, and Erik Brynjolfsson, "Big Data: The Management Revolution," *Harvard Business Review*, Vol. 90, No. 10, 2012, pp. 2–9.

McClave, James T., and Terry T. Sincich, *Statistics*, London: Pearson, 2012.

Mullainathan, Sendhil, and Jann Spiess, "Machine Learning: An Applied Econometric Approach," *Journal of Economic Perspectives*, Vol. 31, No. 2, 2017, pp. 87–106.

Nickerson, David W., and Todd Rogers, "Political Campaigns and Big Data," *Journal of Economic Perspectives*, Vol. 28, No. 2, 2014, pp. 51–74.

Office of Management and Budget, "Privacy Act Implementation: Guidelines and Responsibilities," *Federal Register*, Vol. 40, No. 132, July 9, 1975, pp. 28948–28978. As of July 11, 2019:
https://obamawhitehouse.archives.gov/sites/default/files/omb/assets/omb/inforeg/implementation_guidelines.pdf

Office of Management and Budget, *Guidance for Online Use of Web Measurement and Customization Technologies*, OMB M-10-22, Washington, D.C., June 25, 2010.

Office of Management and Budget, *Managing Information as a Strategic Resource*, Circular No. A-130, Washington, D.C., July 28, 2016a. As of July 11, 2019: https://obamawhitehouse.archives.gov/sites/default/files/omb/assets/OMB/circulars/a130/a130revised.pdf

Office of Management and Budget, *Federal Agency Responsibilities for Review, Reporting, and Publication Under the Privacy Act*, Circular No. A-108, Washington, D.C., December 2016b. As of July 11, 2019: https://www.whitehouse.gov/sites/whitehouse.gov/files/omb/circulars/A108/omb_circular_a-108.pdf

OMB—*See* Office of Management and Budget.

Privacy Act of 1974—*See* U.S. Code, Title 5, Section 552a.

Rahimi, Ali, and Ben Recht, "Reflections on Random Kitchen Sinks," *Arg Min Blog*, 2017. As of July 11, 2019: http://www.argmin.net/2017/12/05/kitchen-sinks/

Ridgeway, Greg, "Policing in the Era of Big Data," *Annual Review of Criminology*, Vol. 1, 2017, pp. 401–419.

Roepe, Lisa Rabasca, "Millennialize Your Recruiting," *HR Magazine*, Vol. 62, No. 3, 2017, pp. 44–48.

Saggi, Mandeep Kaur, and Sushma Jain, "A Survey Towards an Integration of Big Data Analytics to Big Insights for Value-Creation," *Information Processing and Management*, Vol. 54, No. 5, September 2018, pp. 758–790.

Salesforce, "Salesforce Overview," briefing provided to RAND, 2017a.

Salesforce, "Salesforce Recruiting POV," briefing provided to RAND, 2017b.

Segall, Daniel O., *The Use of Social Media in DoD Recruiting and Screening: Exploring Legal, Ethical, and Methodological Issues*, Washington, D.C.: Defense Personal Assessment Center, Office of People Analytics, U.S. Department of Defense, 2018.

Sharda, Ramesh, Dursun Delen, and Efraim Turban, *Business Intelligence, Analytics, and Data Science: A Managerial Perspective*, New York: Pearson Education, Inc., 2018.

Sivarajah, Uthayasankar, Muchammad Mustafa Kamal, Zahir Irani, and Vishanth Weerakkody, "Critical Analysis of Big Data Challenges and Analytical Methods," *Journal of Business Research*, Vol. 70, 2017, pp. 263–286.

Smashfly Technologies, "Man + Machine: The Fundamentals of AI for Recruiting," YouTube, July 26, 2017. As of July 15, 2019: https://www.youtube.com/watch?v=ZeVzzALdEHI

Strazzulla, Phil, "The Best Around: The Top 100 Applicant Tracking Systems in Talent Today," *Recruiting Daily*, April 2017.

U.S. Air Force, briefing shared with RAND, 2018.

U.S. Code, Title 5, Section 552a, Records Maintained on Individuals, December 31, 1974.

U.S. Code, Title 10, Section 503, Enlistments: Recruiting Campaigns; Compilation of Directory Information, January 3, 2012.

U.S. Department of Defense, *Department of Defense Privacy Program*, DoD Regulation 5400.11-R, May 14, 2007.

U.S. Department of Defense, *DoD Privacy Program*, DoD Directive 5400.11, October 29, 2014.

U.S. Department of Defense, *DoD Internet Services and Internet-Based Capabilities*, DoD Instruction 8550.01, Section f(1)(b), "Web Measurement and Customization Technologies," September 11, 2012.

U.S. Department of Justice, *Overview of the Privacy Act of 1974*, 2015 edition, 2015. As of July 11, 2019:
https://www.justice.gov/opcl/file/793026/download

Winston, Wayne L., *Operations Research: Applications and Algorithms*, Boston, Mass.: Cengage Learning, 2003.

Wooldridge, Jeffrey M., *Econometric Analysis of Cross Section and Panel Data*, Boston, Mass.: MIT Press, 2010.

CPSIA information can be obtained
at www.ICGtesting.com
Printed in the USA
LVHW080800211119
638022LV00012B/1047/P

9 781977 403421